Boy of the Wealden Shore

a Hastings Boyhood
1940-1960

by

Derek Booth

Derek Booth

First published in 2011 by Derek Booth

Copyright © Derek Booth

Email: booth30@btinternet.com

ISBN 978-0-9569026-0-3

A catalogue record of this book is available from the British Library.

Printed in Great Britain by

impression IT
Unit 2
Maunsell Road
St Leonards - on - Sea
East Sussex
TN38 9NL

Tel: +44 (0) 1424 852116

www.impressionit.co.uk

Dedication

to the memory of my grandparents and parents who gave me the opportunity to grow up in Hastings on the Wealden shore and to my schoolteachers, notably Tom Cookson and Douglas Brightmore at the Hastings Grammar School who provided me with an education and further opportunities. My dedication extends to the present, to my wife Judith for her continuous support during a long married life and the pleasure of our two daughters Rebecca and her family, and Catherine. Also to the memory of our eldest daughter Amanda whose short presence denied her those experiences of this life.

"We must not forget the natural world because as a species dependent on its resources we are part of it"

Contents

A note on illustrations

All the photographs other than those in the possession of Sarah Sables, Piers Dudgeon and Brian Newbery who have granted permission to reproduce their photographs, are in the possession of the author taken by him, his family, friends and associates. The smallest black and white photographs were taken with a 1930's Kodak 'Brownie' camera.

Reproduced watercolour and oil paintings were either painted by the author, or others as indicated with their permission.

The sketch map of Hoad's Wood and the following 'cartoon' sketches were drawn by the author: Palmated newts in a 'duck pond'; the Hungarian marsh frog emerges; 'East-Enders' relaxing in a deck chair; "What do you think of my 'Andros' after shave dear?"

Acknowledgements

Many years after I had left Hastings, I had contact with Tom and Catherine Cookson who encouraged me to write about my reflections on growing up in Hastings, and that some of my poetry would appropriately support my thoughts and experiences of the simple every day life of those times. I wish to acknowledge this encouragement as a tribute to the inspiration provided by the respective contributions made by this husband and wife team to me, and to our culture through the writings of Catherine Cookson in the 20th century.

I am also grateful for the friendship and shared experiences I had over many years with Barry Kent in the social context of our childhood. Later this was extended to Bob Finch (sadly no longer with us), and Brian Newbery for our shared experiences during and after our attendance at the Hastings Grammar School; all these friends have enabled me to have more substance in the stories I recall in this book. I particularly wish to thank Brian Newbery for providing some of the illustrations with a personal artistic touch, and background literature to expand the geographical and historical aspect of the book. I also wish to thank Sarah Sables and Piers Dudgeon for permission to reproduce photographs from Piers' biography of Catherine Cookson, 'Kate's Daughter' (the real Catherine Cookson), and The Epworth Press for being able to reproduce some of Muriel Hilton's poems.

Bob Finch's cousin John Finch, another ex-Hastings Grammar School boy, is a recent acquaintance and I am grateful to him for the information he has provided on the current water supply to Hastings.

I particularly wish to acknowledge the love and support of my wife Judith, who with our daughters accompanied me on many visits to Hastings over the years.

Thanks are also due to Dr Chris Thomas of Milton Contact Ltd for his profound advice on publishing and editing matters.

Finally, I am most grateful for the encouragement and advice received from Victoria Seymour who has paved the way in Hastings with her books on the social history of people in the town when they were young, or not so young during the 2nd World War and afterwards – so complementary to my own stories.

Preface

The background theme of this book is growing up in the 1940's and 50's in Hastings on the Wealden shore of the Sussex coast. Although the core of the story is autobiographical, an essential feature is the 'boy's' progress through childhood set in the context of social history of a historical, seaside town and surrounding countryside, during and after the Second World War.

The uncertainty of war spent with mother and grandparents is realized as bombs including 'doodlebugs' fall out the sky, but there are moments of tranquility taking walks and picnics into the Wealden countryside. Then this traumatic period in our history dissolves away to peace time as the family is reunited with father returning from military service to establish the needs of running a home. With little money and dependent upon public transport, the family finds pleasure in simple leisure activities, notably days out at the seaside, picnics in the countryside with refreshment at tea rooms, and appreciating the town's cultural attributes – parks, historic buildings and streets, carnivals etc.; walking is essential to the experience.

The 'boy's' progress with age is vividly recalled through playing in local woods and farmland where an interest in natural history is seeded with healthy exercise a bonus. Interest in the natural world is cultivated through secondary education, when the 'boy' attends the Hastings Grammar School. Here, a teacher and neighbour, Tom Cookson husband of the well-known, author Catherine Cookson, is a great inspiration for the 'boy'. Fishing trips on father's old bicycle, accompanied by Barry a childhood friend, widen the 'boy's' exposure to nature and the landscape, but the 'boy' also becomes involved in what the town has to offer a teenager - jazz and becoming a guitar player with the 1066 Skiffle Group (achieving some fame on the South Coast before the

Beatles!). On leaving school, the 'boy' takes a summer vacation employment as a deck chair attendant, an occupation recalled with unique stories, which provides extra income during the 3 years at Hull University studying and obtaining a degree in zoology.

After university, although the 'boy' is offered the post of assistant biology master to Doug Brightmore his past biology master at the Hastings Grammar School, he declines, to continue as a research assistant at University College Hospital Medical School, London, in human fertility, (assisted in turn in the laboratory, by Diana sister of past Chancellor of the Exchequer, Nigel Lawson and aunt of celebrity cook Nigella). While here, the 'boy' marries Judith, a Hull history graduate before moving to Cambridge, where they have three daughters. In Cambridge the 'boy' is employed at an Agricultural Research Council Unit known as the Animal Research Station where pioneering work related to animal breeding and human fertility, was carried out on sperm freezing, in vitro fertilization, embryos (eventually leading to 'Dolly' the sheep) and oral contraception; the 'boy' was awarded a PhD for his work on reproduction in the pig.

In retirement, the 'boy' becomes involved and promotes the novel enterprise of wild boar farming, but ironically some animals with no association with the 'boy', escape (after the October gales of 1987 demolished fencing), to the woods of East Sussex to establish a colony in the countryside of the 'boy's' childhood; the first presence of this beast in the wild of Britain again for several centuries. The 'boy' also has the opportunity to write a book with two previous colleagues on 'A History of the Cambridge Animal Research Station'.

Archaeology, local history, and gardening are some of the interests highlighted in the final chapter as the now 'old boy' continues to live well beyond the Wealden shore, on the fen edge of Cambridgeshire with memories of Hastings where now many of the woods, fields, the Memorial clock at the hub of the town centre, the Central Cricket Ground, the Pier, salt water baths, and the Grammar School, to name a few features of the town over 50 years ago, have sadly gone.

1. Uncertain Times

I gasped my first breath sometime around 6 pm on 18 March 1940 in a bedroom of an unremarkable 1930's rented bungalow situated in suburban Oakdale on the outskirts of Poole, Dorset. My mother Peggy of medium height, attractive with brunette, 1930's bobbed hair and fringe, and hazel eyes, was not quite 22 years old. But, Peggy was over 120 miles from her home town Hastings in East Sussex and her parents could not just drop in from 'round the corner' to witness the new arrival in the family and give immediate support to my mother with her first born child, chubby and bald apart from a few blond hairs. My father Bill was 25 years old and just under 6 feet tall with dark hair, fine features and blue eyes; he was an appropriate match for my mother. However, my father was not going to be around much either in those first few months of my life, or even for the next 5 years – the Second World War had started just 6 months earlier on 3 September 1939, a day that anyone old enough to digest the news on the wireless, chillingly remembers well. But what was I doing here in Poole? Admittedly, it is on the South Coast with the Purbeck hills nearby, but not the Weald of East Sussex that highly wooded landscape known in Roman times as the great forest of Anderida where it meets the English Channel at Hastings; a rich source of iron ore and timber for house and boat building in earlier times.

Like many young men developing a career in their mid – 20's, for my father, his life was going to be a retail tailor with Hepworths and this was his employment in Hastings when he married my mother in August 1938 at Park Road Methodist Church, St Leonards - on - Sea. My father was seeking a manager's post and this became available at Hepworths in the High Street, Poole during the summer of 1939, and so my father and mother emigrated west along the south coast to Poole where my father started his new job and me at the same time; another generation had been conceived.

Once that dreadful protracted War had started, young married couples like my parents, many with young children or expecting them, had the aspirations of their young age shattered by the international tragedy. My father was soon 'called up' to join the Dorset regiment with the main barracks at Dorchester, the county town and the training grounds on the Purbeck Hills near Corfe Castle. However, my father did not remain with the 'Dorsets' for long and transferred to the Military Police giving him the opportunity to be involved with the movement of troops involving map reading, route planning and the use of a BSA motor bike for the remainder of the War. Three years later on 6 June 1944, my father landed on Gold beach towards the evening of D-Day and during the next year he would arrive eventually in Berlin to see the liberation of this battle torn city by the combined allied forces. Although my father was not fighting on the front line, he must have witnessed many poignant events of war which he was hesitant to recall.

My mother not being a particularly adventurous woman, soon felt the stress of isolation in suburban Poole, with my father away except for short durations of leave and her parents and most of the extended family residing in Hastings; my mother's and my time in Poole was short lived. The summer of 1941 and me now a year old, saw my mother and I leave 'Starbrace', the bungalow in Oakdale, Poole for Hastings in East Sussex - back to the homeland to stay temporarily with my maternal grandparents James in Hastings, who lived at the top of Parker Road in another 1930's dwelling, a semi-detached house.

Grandmother James born in 1877 and married in 1902, was a Coalbran, an old Hastings family involved in a variety of every day occupations. Grandfather James' parents and grandparents came from Poplar, Middlesex in the east of London near the East

India docks. His grandfather John James senior was a mariner of humble rank in Nelson's navy and one time steward to Lady Hamilton, Nelson's mistress. John James' son John junior was first a clerk on the docks and later a plate glass cutter, carver and gilder moving to Hastings for a second marriage at All Saints Church in 1868 which produced my grandfather in 1879 when John was 63. John James junior was an interesting person from a complex family context, and I wonder whether his move to Hastings led to him becoming involved with the many artists who visited the town such as the Pre-Raphaelites Daniel Rosseti and Holman Hunt, making their picture frames; a framed oil portrait of John James junior may have been a gift from an artist who had frames made by my great grandfather, and he made the frame for his own portrait. All this is speculation and research is needed to confirm or refute these possibilities.

Both my maternal grandparents were keen gardeners. Grandmother James nursed the flowers visible in the small front garden with more trailing on terraces in the steep sloping back garden which included fruit bushes and trees. Among the fruit trees, notably were greengage, Victoria and Golden plums; my first taste of these delicious oval fruits, picked direct from the trees eaten then or cooked for a dessert. At the bottom of the garden was a greenhouse where grandfather James grew those wonderful tomatoes smelling like tomatoes of yester-years and the wire netting door to keep out any birds tempted by the red ripening fruit. Through the arched gateway in the green privet hedge was grandfather's pride and joy, his allotment with a chicken run and a handful of laying hens. Here also were four fattening cockerels, one for each of his three married children including my mother and one for Parker Road, this tradition carried on for several years after the War.

Grandfather James was a very practical man. In addition to constructing chicken runs and house, a garden shed and miniature garden, grandfather James dug out the earth from under the kitchen for an air raid shelter with steps leading down to it. Fortunately the hard concrete bunks in the shelter were never needed, but the new 'cellar' made a convenient extra store for garden materials including old sacks – I shall never forget that musty, earthy smell of hessian and stale air. Other examples of grandfather James' practical skills were the making a four roomed doll's house (in the style of a Victorian house where my mother was born in 1918 in Victoria Avenue), complete with electric lights for my mother when she was a child. But for me it was a large wooden steam engine to sit on when I was about 4 years old, and because it had wheels I could manoeuvre this large toy with my feet around the house or garden; it was painted green and black representing a Southern Railway engine. The second toy on wheels which I could sit on and shuffle around with my feet, was a joint product of grandfather and grandmother James ingenuity, it was an elephant. Grandfather built the wooden frame and fixed the wheels, while grandmother did the upholstery, padding out the skeleton of wood and covering all with grey flannel to look like elephant skin; white cloth, padded tusks were sown on as were glass eyes and a maroon and gold saddle. I played with these magnificant home made toys well into my first years at school after the War.

Being a practical man, grandfather James started his working life as a white smith working with soft metals such as tin and copper (there were a number of examples of his work around the house) before being employed as an electrician with the early Hastings Electric Light Company; grandfather eventually became a mains foreman. The Electric Works were in Earl Street next to the railway and grandfather and grandmother James lived nearby in Mann Street before moving to Parker Road in 1936 when the new Power Station came into operation in Ore Valley. Related to the fact that grandfather James worked in the electrical industry, this literally put grandmother James 'on the stage' as the first woman in

Hastings to cook with an electric stove at a public demonstration.

Head on to grandfather's allotment down hill, was another tilled by Doug Brightmore, a biology master at the Hastings Grammar School who one day would set me on the path to a career as a research biologist. Doug also lived in a 1930's semi-detached house on the neighbouring road west of Parker Road called Hoad's Wood Road. Immediately next door and down hill from the Brightmore's was the Hurst, home of Tom Cookson, a maths master at the Grammar School and his wife Catherine, one day to become one of the most poplar novelists of social history in the 20th century with her stories on the raw life of her childhood background in Jarrow on Tyne side.

Looking through the French windows of my grandparents dining room revealed a panoramic view, to the west with dramatic sunsets, over the garden and allotments to the tower on the Hurst (a typical feature of late Victorian architecture) in mid-view, and across a valley to a hill which was capped by a long rectangular, pink brick building known as Ore Place. This building was once a seminary where the polymath Pierre Teilhard de Chardin trained to become a Jesuit priest between 1908 and 1911. Teilhard de Chardin (1881-1955) was a theologian, philosopher and a paleontologist who used to break open rocks with his geological hammer to expose fossils along the shore where the Sussex Weald meets the coast at Ecclesbourne and Fairlight glens. *This rugged and wind-swept part of the Wealden shore was later to have a great impact on me, enthralled by such natural environs.* Teilhard de Chardin was a pioneer in attempting to bring together those 'opposing' disciplines of science and religion; his philosophical thinking welded the evolution of the physical universe with biological evolution on our planet which led to the human species – all was unity created by God which led to his classic book 'The Phenomenon of Man'.

This was the setting of my grandparents house but where were my mother and I going to live? In uncertain times, there was one certainty, my mother and I were to live in yet another 1930's semi-detached house at the bottom of Hoad's Wood Road where the road levels out. My grandfather had noticed that no.18 was to let and with approval all round, this was to be the family home for the next 60 years; in 1951 my parents had the opportunity to buy the property as 'sitting tenants'.

Because of my young age, there are only a few events I can recall of those traumatic War years, particularly of the War itself. While on the one hand children were being evacuated, including the Hastings Grammar School to St Albans from areas like Hastings which were on the front line geographically in relation to the main confrontation happening over on the Continent, my mother and I made ourselves potentially more vulnerable moving to Hastings. This can be seen from a map showing where the bombs fell in Hastings and St Leonards resulting in 150 locals losing their lives and over 700 injured, 260 seriously. Fortunately for my mother and I and other relatives living in Hastings, we all survived without injury.

Those War related instances I can recall, are as follows. The first, though dramatic to a 3 year old was not directly War related yet in a way it was. During the summer of 1943, my mother, her childhood friend Joy and her half brother Bill Warren (an ex-Hastings Grammar School boy) took me on a picnic to Fairlight Cove, a dip in the Wealden hills on the coast east of Fairlight glen about 3 miles from Hastings. While we were there, one of those violent thunderstorms that brew up on a hot summer's day over the English Channel, menacingly moved over us whereupon we were forced to take shelter on the verandah of a deserted chalet; there was just a handful of these summer residences, a few houses and a hotel which constituted a hamlet at the Cove (today the area is a substantial suburban complex). The story ends with torrential rain and the rotting wooden seat we were sitting on suddenly collapsing under our weight and me being buried under bodies larger than mine!

Bill Warren was on leave as a flight engineer on Lancaster bombers with 115 Squadron based at Witchford near Ely, Cambridgeshire (about 12 miles from where I live today). Sadly, Bill was shot down in a Lancaster over Germany in March 1944 after carrying out a bombing raid on Berlin; he was only 22. Bill was engaged to be married later that spring and fatefully had volunteered to go into the air force without obligation because he was employed in an essential service in civilian life working as an office worker for the Maidstone & District Motor Services Ltd. Bill is buried at Oberkirchen in Germany and his name is entered in a memorial book at Ely Cathedral. The circumstances and events of the loss of the aircraft and crew are reported in a small museum on an industrial estate near the original runway for the squadron at Witchford; the survival of one of the crew is remarkable. The Lancaster Mk2 bomber was shot down by a German Ju 88. Four crew including Bill were lost, but 3 of the remaining 7 crew survived and were taken as prisoners of war. One of these survivors, Sergeant Nicholas Alkemade fell 18,000 feet and his fall was broken by thick snow on the branches of a tree, he died over 40 years later in 1987.

Another occasion when adults protectively piled on top of me, was while I was travelling back to Hastings from Dunmow, Essex with my mother; her sister had given birth to her third child, a daughter in July 1944. My mother and I were on the London Underground at Aldgate station when a German V1 flying bomb, the dreaded 'doodlebug' landed close to the station with an unforgettable explosion – soldiers in uniform and my mother cocooned me on the floor of the carriage, a close shave but no one was hurt on the train. Closer to home a 'doodlebug' landed near to my grandparents James' house on the edge of a field by the side of the road in Pine Avenue; the twisted iron carcass laid there for many

10

years after the War. Every time I walked by, I had a morbid fascination to peer over the fence into the field and glance at the twisted metal carcass as though it was a skeleton of some unknown monster.

A direct hit by one of these flying bombs fortunately did not occur, but there was widespread damage from the terrific blast of an exploding 'doodlebug' nearby, breaking many windows and dismantling chimney pots over a wide area; the up stairs ceilings at our house in Hoad's Wood Road were repaired with plaster board overlay. It was not always enemy material that fell out of the sky. Two Polish fighter planes collided over Ravine Lodge near our house in Hoad's Wood Road. Years later when I was playing in Hoad's Wood, I found a tin of live bullets which must have arisen from the planes during collision, needless to say my father took them to the police station. Just inland from Fairlight glen near North Seat (named after an earlier MP for Hastings) and the highest hill on the Wealden shore at over 170m, was a search light station and anti-aircraft guns. I can clearly recall seeing the beams at night from the search lights, from Hoad's Wood Road as they scanned the sky to the east for enemy aircraft.

The unpleasant incidences of the War to the uncontaminated mind of a child are by contrast clearly remembered, but their significance is not put into the perspective of being out of the ordinary as is the awareness of the adult mind. Equally however, I have memories of the War which transcend to peace time. Among these were walking to St. Helen's Church on a Sunday morning with my mother and grandparents James from the gravel surface of their end of Parker Road to the junction of St. Helen's Down Road with Hoad's Wood Road and Pilot Road lined by gorse bushes. All these roads were unadopted without tarmac, just rough quarry stones and grassy patches and few houses; you felt you had already travelled into the countryside. At the top of Pilot Road we turned left along The Ridge, the boundary road of

Hastings running along the ridge of the Wealden hill which progresses from the old village of Ore to the small town of Battle of 1066 fame; this was the earlier route from the old town of Hastings to London and known as the Old London Road. On our right was the extensive borough cemetery; (it is only recently that I found out that grandfather James father, John James junior and his first wife originally from the dock lands of East London are buried together near the wall of the cemetery which runs along the main road, The Ridge; this is one of the earliest graves in the cemetery dated 1868 to 1882). About a couple of hundred yards from here on a bend is St. Helen's Church. As we were approaching the church and meeting others going to the same destination, grandfather James walking on the kerb side of grandmother, her right arm tucked into his left arm, would politely lift his trilby hat by its crown in his right hand, to ladies, this was part of the etiquette of life then; (today, fewer men or woman wear hats for such customary behaviour).

At the church, we were allocated a family pew near the front of the nave on the left; grandfather James was a churchwarden receiving the collection on this side of the nave. Also on this north side of the church sat girls with their purple brimmed hats from St. Margaret's boarding school which was directly across the road from the church, while on the south side of the church were boys attired in conventional grey suits from Hurst Court, a preparatory school the next site along the The Ridge on the other side of Chown's Hill; the head master Mr Curtis sometimes used to assist in the service, (both schools have long ceased to exist). This experience on a Sunday morning was my first exposure to the liturgy of the Church of England instilling in me for all time the Anglican order of service, and universal hymns of the Christian religion. However, I was too young to remember the content of the sermons delivered by the Rev. Graham, no doubt they reflected on how one can reconcile war and peace. The organist was Mr Gasson, a serious looking man with horn rimmed glasses, and air for the organ pipes was pumped by hand. The caretaker was Mr Wilson, a dapper man with a long waxed moustache, a left over from a military fashion earlier in the century, and what little auburn hair was left on his head, this was plastered down with 'Brylcream'. Mr Wilson lived in the house which was part of the Sunday school complex next to the church, which I was later to attend where the teacher was Mrs Joan Tidmarsh and the Rev. King the new rector. In my teen years, I graduated from Sunday school to bible class held at the rectory further along The Ridge on the right beyond the girls' High School (today the former rectory is now a nursing home).

On another day of the week before the end of the War, and the weather was fine, my mother, grandparents James and I would walk pass St. Helen's Church and descend off the Wealden ridge down Stonestile Lane in the direction of the village of Westfield, about 2 miles away. Instead of hymn books and bibles, we would be carrying old canvas bags full of scrambled egg sandwiches and grandfather's sumptuous tomatoes; bottles of orange juice and a thermos flask of hot tea would wash this down once we found a picnic spot. After a mile or so this welcome spot would arise as the lane levelled out to a small valley with a scintillating stream draining the Wealden hills behind; the stream passed under a stone bridge further down the lane. Before descending into this dip in the landscape, if it was spring, we had passed the many clumps of primroses cascading down the steep banks at the side of the lane, these clumps of early fragrance were kept moist by small springs issuing from the clay soil, prevented from retention by the sandstone subsoil. As we approached the stream, it was bordered by a hazel copse which in turn was separated from the lane by a narrow meadow. Here the cool copse would be carpeted with blue bells, white wood anemones and the opposing pungent odour of the wild garlic or ransomes, near the stream; this left an indelible olfactory memory on the nostrils. During one of these picnics, grandfather James cut a hazel stick from the copse so that like him

I had a walking stick to help me on my way back up the lane for the return journey home, but being only 3 or 4 years old, did I need a walking stick at this tender age? I think not, it is more likely that I swung the stick aimlessly over the invasive bracken in the meadow!

An alternative picnic route was to walk the Iron Bridge circuit of around 2-3 miles. starting by walking up Pine Avenue, crossing The Ridge and descending down Ivy House Lane so named because of he ivy clad farmhouse along the lane. After awhile we would leave the lane and go through a stile on the right, across a field and over the track running from The Ridge to Coghurst Hall, an early 19th century house built in 1811 by the Brisco family; (today it is a caravan site). Grandfather James when he was a young man working for the Hastings Electric Light Company, was involved in installing the first electric lights at Coghurst Hall. With the track behind us, we settled down to our usual picnic menu at a spot at the edge of a field facing south, so that my mother and I could lay back in the sun after the meal while the grandparents more sedately sat upright, possibly lost in thought of earlier days here when my mother was a child. After this welcome rest, we set off for the Iron Bridge, a foot bridge over the Hastings to Ashford railway line which in those days conveyed passenger trains powered by a steam engine. My mother told me that when she was a child being taken for a walk in this area, she saw a swallow tail butterfly, a rarity today confined mostly to some fenland reserves of Cambridgeshire and the Norfolk Broads.

The other side of the Iron Bridge, led to a footpath winding up through woodland to Rock Lane where we sometimes paused at an old cottage to buy apples from a Mrs Standen, possibly a distant relative; the cider smell of the apples ripening in a brick floored out house, left another olfactory memory. The circular picnic excursion was completed by walking down Winchelsea Road from where you could see the sea beyond the main town of Hastings, then into Ore village and along The Ridge to Pine Avenue, passing the gatehouse at the start of the track to Coghurst Hall. This gatehouse had grey hounds embossed in stone over the gateway, (the gateway was demolished many years ago). The Iron Bridge circuit would often be walked in late summer to pick the prolific harvest of blackberries in the hedgerows. Another use for grandfather's walking stick was to grab those unreachable runners, always with the largest berries, so that they could be picked; these fruits of nature would be converted into jam or jelly by grandmother or mother. An alternative venue for these musky fruits was closer to Hoad's Wood Road, the hedgerows separating Langham Road from fields once part of Oakwood House; I can remember the ruined cellars. (Over 50 years ago these fields were built on, adding to the suburban sprawl as Oakwood Close, the development was mostly bungalows where later I would do a paper round).

Although my father was away for most of the time on military service during the War, he like others in the forces came home on leave from time to time. One of my earliest memories was Christmas 1943 when I was 3 years old and father was on leave for the festive occasion that year. I must have been so excited not just because Father Christmas was going to come down the chimney to give me a big pillow case of presents, after I had put out biscuits and milk for his reindeers, but because my real father was to be the Christmas father this year. I recall getting out of bed, creeping stealthily down the stairs and sitting on the old Victorian chaise longue in the dining room (the remaining part of the Victorian suite was at Parker Road where grandfather James sat in the larger chair with arms, to the right of the dining room fireplace, and grandmother sat in the smaller, armless, ladies chair placed on the left of the fireplace). It was very cold sitting on this simulated leather 'bed' and the dying embers in the basket-like Sussex grate emitted only the faintest glow. Suddenly father and mother opened the dining room door, *"What are you doing out of bed this time of day, it is 3 o'clock in the morning!"* Quivering white with cold and embarrassment, I said, *"I was waiting for Father Christmas"*, but really it was comforting to see my real father again. I knew he was coming home, hence the added excitement, but my father arrived home on leave after I had gone to bed the previous evening. My parents were obviously so pleased that the three of us were all together again, however brief, and told me to go back to bed otherwise Father Christmas would pass by our house. I soon went up those stairs, fell asleep and awoke at a more civilized time to see the pillow case bulging with irregular shapes by the fireplace - an unforgettable Christmas.

Uncertainty of the War years became a certainty for me in the spring of 1945, I started full time education in the summer term after my fifth birthday in March. My first school was St. Andrew's Church of England primary school in Stonefield Road which my mother had attended 20 years earlier when she lived at Mann Street near her father's work at the Electric Works in Earl Street. In my first year at the school, I remember drawing pin men like all children do, but additionally reflecting the times, I also remember drawing 'doodlebugs' – a cigar shaped body with a smaller 'cigar' above the tail end spurting forth flames! This artistic effort exhausted us, which led to the class having a siesta on oval coconut mats individually collected from a wooden chest; building bricks were nearby in a similar chest. Towards the end of the school day in the winter months when the light was dimming, the teacher would light a wax taper with a match and insert it under the white glass shade of a gas light in the middle of the class room – after a few 'pops' the gas ignited. We could then carry on writing 'Jack and Jill went up the hill' after dipping our pen nibs, fixed to a wooden shaft into the black ink contained in the white china wells lodged in the old wooden desks – all was unchanged since the school was built in Victorian times. Interestingly, there was a teacher with the name none other than Miss Inkpen!

The school was not far from St. Andrew's Church in Queen's Road where the school went to a service on St. Andrew's Day. Within the church, the notable Robert Tressell pseudonym of Robert Noonan, had produced some colorful panels and he was the author of 'The Ragged Trousered Philanthropists', a story about the hard life of working people in 'Mugsborough' (actually Hastings) early in the 20th century. One time this interesting person lived in a house in Milward Road at the top of the steps leading up from Stonefield Road next to St. Andrew's school (sadly, neither the church nor the school exists today although the latter building exists converted into flats). In 1948 the school was closed due to war damage and I was transferred to Mount Pleasant Junior School.

This period of my life is reflected in the following poem:

'Pipe and Old Sacks'

Four pm Thursday, such a special day,
School bell rings at St. Andrew's, I'm on my way.
Up the steps by the side of the school
Through the heady smell of lilac and elder flower bloom,
Into Milward Road I emerge and wait,
Hoping the No. 72, Maidstone & District won't be late.
"Penny, top of Parker Road", I say to the conductor,
In return I receive a penny-printed piece of paper.

Ten minutes later I alight at the terminus
With a quarter mile walk up to the semi for all of us;
For here at No. 249,
Lives Granddad, Grandma, maiden Aunt – maternal line.
But the first to give welcome on this warm May evening
Is not the inhabitants,
But the rewards of their laboring.

17

A small front garden neat with shrubs and sweet annuals
First nutured in the greenhouse,
No help from the Manuals.

Through the glass panel in the green back door,
I see Mum, arrived just an hour before.
I enter the kitchen so homely for me
As Mum, Grandma, Aunt Marjorie prepare the tea.
"Where is Granddad?" I ask, though I already know,
He is down the garden where all granddads go.
Nearest the house the back garden is terraced
With two rockeries, bird house, miniature garden – pool
And trellis.

As I descend steps through this ornamental maze,
My next warm greeting is the odour of creosote
And pipe - smoke in the haze.
I open the shed door, it squeeks just a bit -
There's Granddad! - faded grey Trilby, brown jacket, pipe
Over-filled with 'St. Julian's', only half lit.
We have a chat about this and that,
"How did you get on at school today?"
I say, " I drew a black cat"
A pensive moment, Granddad's thumb sparks the flint,
Petrol in his lighter burns, 'St. Julian' gets a glint.

More memorable smoke blended with earthy sacks,
A whiff of hessian, neatly folded in stacks.
"What about an egg for tea?" Granddad chuckles,
So off down the garden we go towards the hen-cackles.
Through a gate in the privet between garden and allotment
We go to the hen yard to seek further contentment,
For there in a nest box cosily lined with straw
Are five of the brownest eggs I ever saw.

Into a saucepan (handle long since gone),
I gingerly place each brown nugget, one by one.
Back in the kitchen, a further homely smell
Freshly brewed tea, home made scones, plum jam as well.
Into another saucepan the warm eggs become warmer,
Four minutes, no more, over the old electric burner.
Five o'clock on the dot, we sit round the table -
'Home Service', Uncle Mac is reading a fable.

Off comes the knitted cosies from teapot and eggs,
Each similar in pattern, quilted squares,
Many colours, including red.
Repeated sound of tea tinkling into bone china cups,
Mellowed with milk and sugar,
Or tanged with lemon for Aunt to sup.
Brown-breaded 'soldiers' spread thick with butter,
I dip them into an orange, yolked egg,
Granddad gives a mutter.
With NHS glasses on forehead, Daily Express in left hand,
"What's Attlee up to now with the rest of his band?"

Too young to respond to such political context,
I gaze through French windows across wooded views
To the sunset.
A stone's throw away in centre view, is the Hurst,
Home to the Cooksons, maths teacher Tom, authoress
Catherine, one day a first.
Next door to them lives rugged Duggy Brightmore,
Another Grammar School master – biology after the War.
I do not know now the importance of these neighbours,
My teachers one day, Catherine's books in the stores.

My final recall of the War years was the Victory (VE) celebrations after the end of the War on 8 May 1945. My mother and an aunt with a cousin took me to Winkle Island in the Old Town one evening for a 'knees up' and I expect in the back streets and passages the pubs were 'running dry'. Another VE celebration was a damp squib for me. Next to my house in Hoad's Wood Road was a vacant plot of land where now, not needed table tops of Morrison air raid shelters were assembled for a street party, but I did not attend – I had German measles (our enemy had the last word!), and it rained and rained. The party I think was held in the dry of Ravine Lodge, one of the few large Victorian houses in Hoad's Wood Road other than the Hurst, the home of the Cooksons, (Ravine Lodge was demolished for a housing development, Ravine Close over 40 years ago). And so the War was ended, I would not have to undergo the claustrophobic rehearsal of putting that rubber gas mask on again, but when would I have my father about the house – full time for the first time in my life?

An emotional response to the War is poignantly captured in the following poem written by my mother 'Peggy' on 26 October 1941 in the new family home at Hoad's Wood Road, and sent to my father 'Bill' on military service.

'On War And Peace'

Once we were happy, you and I,
My dearest love and hearts desire,
We lived in love that's born of God,
Until – the enemy resolved once more
To set the world on fire.

What joy was ours the day our son was born,
You came to me when that small strife was o'er,
And held my hand and helped to comfort me,

20

And help me on the road to health once more.

As I sit here beside our fire alone,
I think of you and oh! The joy it brings!
When I shall hear your step along the road,
And the house once more with laughter rings!

Those treasured days of leave,
When just we three are glad to be alive
To live and breath, and snatch forgotten happiness
'Ere on the road we go once more to strive.

And when alone at night I lay and think of days ahead,
When you and I will once more parted be,
I pray to God that all the heart aches and the fears
Will be atoned when you return to me.

For in my heart I know that day will surely dawn,
When all the world will cease to run with blood,
And then the devilish enemy shall sink to shame,
And their evil powers perish in the mud.
And so I wait with patience, hope and faith,
Upon the day when you my love come home to me,
And watch our son grow up,
And oh! My dear! How happy we will be!

© Joyce Marguerite Booth

L to R: mother, grandfather Booth, father

seated – grandmother Booth with Derek in 1941

(at Park View Clinic, Bohemia, St. Leonards)

Derek at picnic spot in Stonestile Lane with hazel stick cut by

grandfather James in 1943

grandmother and grandfather James at Parker Road, late 1930's

view from grandparents James' house in Parker Road across allotments.

Hoad's Wood in middle distance with Blacklands to Bohemia and Silverhill,

St. Leonards in far distance, late 1930's

(the Cookson's house the 'Hurst' is just out the picture to the right)

Garden of the Cookson's house the 'Hurst' in 1946.

Catherine Cookson is on the right, her cousin Sarah Sables is on the left.

The author's grandparents James' house in Parker Road is visible through the trees

at the top right of the photograph.

2. Father - Home at Last

My father had to stay on with the Military Police in Berlin after the official end of the War in May 1945. For the remainder of that year, my father along with thousands of other military personnel had to assist with getting Berlin on its feet after the appalling destruction and innocent loss of life it suffered towards the end of the War. During my father's time in Berlin several photographs were taken including the Reichstag (which now has been restored as Germany's parliament building), the Brandenburg Gate and the Victory Monument to the Franco – Prussian War in the 19th century. There were also many photographs of my father called by his buddies 'General' (although he only had the rank of corporal), after William Booth the founder of the Salvation Army because his name was William Booth; my first name is also William.

Before my father left Berlin to return home permanently, he had had many experiences like most service men after landing on the Normandy beaches and eventually reaching Berlin; however there are just two I wish to recall. While passing through Lille in northern France, one evening my father got into conversation with a French school master on a bridge, his name was Paul Roland. Every summer for 10 years after the War until he died in 1956, Paul stayed at our home in Hoad's Wood Road so that he could improve his English as well as keeping up the friendship with my father and the rest of our family. Monsieur Roland would make trips into Hastings on the no. 75 Maidstone & District, double decker bus and get talking to people in public places i.e. on the bus, in sun shelters on the promenade and in Alexandra Park. A most likeable man, Paul Roland made a few more lasting friends through the casual contacts in town and brought over from France many examples of particular French food and liqueurs; this was our own experience of 'entente cordiale'.

When my father arrived in Berlin and met the Russians advancing from the opposite direction, he went into the derelict Olympic Stadium where the games were held in 1936, notable for the fact that the non-white runner Jessie Owen from the USA was a star performer; needless to say Adolf Hitler was not impressed! In the basement of the Stadium were memorabilia of the games including archery equipment (I had the opportunity 50 years later to visit the stadium and witness the restoration of one of the few positive creations of the Nazi regime).

On two occasions when my father returned home on leave from Germany, he brought home in his 'kit bag' first a German radio set, usable in England, then most memorable to me a German train set consisting of two large and very heavy clockwork steam engines, a coal tender, two carriages each equiped with seats and toilets – such detail, flip over destination board (Hamburg, Nurnberg, Warsaw, Leipzig etc.) and of course a selection of large gauge rail sections compared with our Hornby equivalents. How all this was crammed into a 'kit bag' seems remarkable to me – the rail tracks were extensive enough to link round the garden forming a sort of model railway. What happened to that railway set, I do not know. My father probably took it, and another clockwork toy, a model German fighter plane he brought home for me, to one of the many second hand shops in Hastings in exchange for a sum of money that today would be well below the market value, considering these toys, and the radio were all received from German citizens in exchange for packets of service allowance cigarettes which my father did not smoke.

January 1946 and my father was home for good, that year for the first time since I was born he could become a real husband and father. The first thing my father had to do was to get a job, his pre-war occupation as a retail tailor was not available in Hastings, therefore as an interim employment, he along with many other ex-servicemen were given employment at the Army Records Office at

Ore Place, a somewhat different function for this building than when it was a Jesuit seminary; this was only about a 20 minute walk from Hoad's Wood Road. Christmas 1946 and I attended a Christmas party at Ore Place for children of employees at the Army Record Office, a photograph of the occasion suggests the party was held in the dining hall of the old seminary where Teilhard de Chardin, the notable French priest mentioned earlier, would have taken his meals.

With some money coming into the household, my father set about getting the garden into shape and with rationing still well in place and not an abundance of food, many people were growing vegetables and keeping chickens as my grandfather James was doing, also my grandfather Booth was growing vegetables at Bohemia, St. Leonards. My father followed the necessary trend, he acquired an old chicken house from an elderly lady living in Elphinstone Road, in Ore valley. I remember my father and I making several journeys to bring back the dismantled chicken house in sections, tied and resting on the pedals of a war grade Raleigh bicycle he had acquired, this bicycle was painted black with no chrome and was later to become my means of getting about the Wealden countryside, a true mechanical work horse and 'friend' taking me to the wonder and landscapes of this corner of south east England.

My father had set up the chicken house and wire netting run with 4 Rhode Island cross Light Sussex hens which took up nearly half of the small back garden leaving little space for growing vegetables, so where was there an allotment? An obvious possibility was a vacant plot near grandfather James allotment, and luckily there was one. To get there was a short cut through Hoad's Wood which bordered the allotments which took the corner off walking up the length of Hoad's Wood Road and taking a footpath to Parker Road. I often accompanied my father to his allotment helping him lift over a fence his white 'kit bag' now with garden tools and not his war time travelling possessions. I cannot remember how long my father had this allotment, probably a year or two because another allotment became available nearer home opposite the Dorset Laundry and adjacent to the BOS (Boys Own Society) field in Elphinstone Road. (Both the allotments and BOS field are still there today, but the laundry with its 'art deco' facade including a clock on a central tower with blue hands and undefined hour numbers was demolished for housing at the end of the last century; the clock was always a reminder when the next bus was coming for town or the time necessary to get to school! Grandfather James and my father's allotments between Hoad's Wood Road and Parker Road have also gone, around 50 years ago and replaced by Linley Drive with its associated houses and bungalows).

The next year 1947 was to witness the coldest Winter for decades followed by a hot Summer. The cold weather did not set in until the end of January when it lasted for 6 weeks into early March, most of Britain was affected. Repetitive alternating periods of heavy snow, thawing rain and freezing conditions led to the accumulation of ice on coniferous trees which were prevalent in Dunclutha Road between Ore Place and Hoad's Wood Road. The weight of the ice caused branches to break off the trees providing a ready supply of firewood, if you had a saw. My father wasted no time in purchasing a bow saw, and he and I set off with that loyal war grade bicycle to saw the fallen branches into lengths that could be strapped on to the cross bar of the bicycle. On reaching home the branches were cut into logs for our open fires, the main source of heat in the house and additionally the closed, coke burning fire ('coffee pot') beneath a hot water tank in the kitchen. But this was insufficient to stop the north easterly winds from freezing the pipes in the bathroom at the front of the house; small paraffin lamps of different colours were placed near the pipes, but these did little to prevent some freezing and subsequent bursting of the old lead pipes.

The beaches on the South coast were again made available to the public at the end of the War after being out of bounds cluttered with a variety of sea defences including concrete tank traps and barbed wire to stall Hitler's army if he had decided to take over Britain; fortunately he decided otherwise and went east to Russia. As mentioned, the hot summer of 1947 was a total contrast to the harsh winter of that year, this meant that my mother, father and I could make our first trips as a family to the seaside; there were three places on the Wealden shore where we dipped our toes in the water and got vitamin D synthesized in our skin without allowing ourselves to get sun burnt. The first was obviously the beach off the promenade at Hastings. Favourite spots were opposite the Queen's Hotel in the centre of town and the beach just west of the Pier at the beginning of Bottle Alley, that unique Hastings feature on the lower promenade where pieces of coloured glass from broken bottles are cemented into the wall, an innovation by Sidney Little in the 1930's.

A second beach venue and most impressive to me, was Pett Level particularly at Cliff End where the Wealden sandstone ends abruptly at the eastern end of the range of cliffs running along the coast from Hastings. Sometimes we walked the whole 6 miles or so from Hoad's Wood Road to Pett Level via Pett village, but if we wanted more time on the beach we would take an East Kent single decker bus from Hastings promenade to Chick Hill, the short hill with a very steep gradient, about 1 in 3 (cars used to struggle to ascend) and walk down the hill into Pett Level. A distinctive annual event which could be seen in Pett village was the presence of those mud constructed nests of the swallow, precariously fixed under the eaves of the post office near the church. The quickest route to Pett Level was to take another East Kent bus which went via Fairlight direct to Pett Level. Pett Level and Chick Hill are one of many eastern extremities of the Wealden hills which end abruptly along an ancient shore line towards Rye interspersed by streams and rivers connecting with the River Rother which surrounds Rye before it meanders out to sea at Rye Harbour.

Anticipating that Napoleon in the early 19th century might invade England, again the south east corner of the country was on the front line. So that our military equipment could be conveyed along the coast, but slightly inland and acting as a 'moat', a canal was dug from Pett Level around the perimeter of Romney Marsh to Hythe in Kent; either side of Rye the Rivers Rother and Brede formed part of the canal system which became known as the Royal Military Canal. Fortunately, as happened a century and a half later, the mind of a potential invader turned away from Britain to Russia and again led to the demise of the aggressor and his army. The military canal today apart from being part of the greater Romney Marsh water catchment system, has a peaceful use as a course fishing venue and haven for wild life together with the surrounding low lying meadows between the lower Wealden hills and the coast, embracing Romney Marsh.

Whichever way we arrived at Pett Level, my parents and I needed some refreshment, particularly if we had walked there before our picnic lunch on the beach. There used to be a chalet up a track set in marsh land at the foot of Chick Hill and at the beginning of the military canal, this was a tea room run by a Mrs (or Miss) Broad. Here we had a cup of tea or coffee, or a soft drink and on one occasion my father bought me one of those metal children's beach buckets painted with a Walt Disney scene on the outside, plus a metal spade with a wooden handle. One of the few plastic implements for children at the seaside in those days, was a windmill you plunged into the sand or shingle and hoped the wind would be strong enough to propel it – that was not usually a problem!

The sea shore at Pett Level has changed considerably in the last 60 years. Today it is mostly a shingle beach which has built up against the sea wall stretching from Pett Level to Winchelsea beach; the extensive accumulation of shingle is due to the west to east Channel current. Cliff End our favourite spot, was, and still is the most diverse natural shore habitat with the minimum of stark shingle. We left the narrow coast road at Pett Level and walked up a track towards Cliff End and on to the shore. At the eastern end of the beach were memorabilia of the War including the conical shaped tank traps which would have been an obstacle to Hitler's army if they had landed. However, these man-made objects were essentially the only features that were not part of the natural landscape. Apart from the beauty of the crumbling, jagged cliffs was the unusual 'chocolate' brown sand dispersed in small areas between rocks as though nature had created for us, individual picnic areas. And so we spread out father's army groundsheet on the brown sand with sand hoppers (shrimp like crustaceans) leaping and escaping from our rude intrusion on their homeland.

When the tide was out, another world was revealed, a terrain of ancient submerged forest remaining as black tree stumps intermingled with rock pools which gave me my first introduction to intertidal fauna and flora including colourful seaweed, anemones, shore crabs, limpets and most importantly winkles – these were food, those small molluscs with dark grey shells and full of flavour. My parents and I would fill my beach bucket with these shore snails after dislodging them from the small rocks around the pools. When we got home my mother would boil the winkles in salted water and after draining off the water and leaving them to cool, we would sit round the kitchen table each armed with a small needle to probe out the winkles from their shells. The winkles were then steeped in vinegar until eaten accompanied by hot buttered toast or brown bread and butter – a simple food for free to add a gourmet touch to our usual 5 o'clock tea of meat dripping or paste on bread followed by cake and listening to Uncle Mac on 'Childrens Hour' on the Home Service.

Because of the rocks, Cliff End was not a good beach for swimming. However, none of us were swimmers and my parents were happy to recline on the brown sand with their exposed skin turning a similar colour without sunburn as their skin was not fair; I was happy to go off and explore the rock pools, an early stimulus to my developing interest in the natural world. This on one occasion was enhanced by the unexpected song of a nightingale produced in the middle of the day from a bird hidden in the small trees along the shore only yards from our home for the day on the beach.

The third beach we visited was west of Hastings, indeed it was the other side of Bexhill at Cooden. To get there, instead of taking a bus it was a special treat to catch a Southern Region electric train from Ore station (a 20 minute walk from Hoad's Wood road),to Cooden beach which was some eight miles from Ore, the train would eventually be going to Brighton or Victoria station in London. Cooden beach is good for bathing being a mixture of shingle and sand, but as a natural habitat it is wind swept and featureless. However, it must have been a popular venue because at the beginning of the 20th century, the Hastings Tramways Company had a route running there from Hastings through St. Leonards and Bexhill and in the late 1920's trolley buses replaced the trams; incidently I have tickets from one of the last trolley bus journeys made on 31 May 1959.

During the next few years, the treat of travelling on the electric train, or a South Down bus from Wellington Square, would take us to Pevensey with its ancient ruined castle of Roman and Norman construction, and the old Mint House (with its ghost!). Further along the line, or road, was Hastings' neighbouring seaside resort (17 miles away) of Eastbourne and the adjacent hills of the South Downs terminating at Beachy Head. My father liked the clean, brightness and predominantly Victorian and Edwardian promenade of Eastbourne with its pier, bandstand and flower gardens. I also accepted this favourable atmosphere, but I preferred the quaintness of the Old Town of Hastings with its little back streets, timber framed houses and the fishing quarters, backed by the Wealden sandstone cliffs. A short bus ride away from Eastbourne, were Wannock Gardens with their tea rooms – father could not resist this extension to the outing.

A final event I can recall of that hot summer of 1947 following one of the coldest winters of the century, was returning to my birth county of Dorset for a fortnight's holiday at the end of August. Our journey involved taking an East Kent coach from Hastings railway station to Portsmouth and transferring to a more luxurious Royal Blue coach for the final part of the journey to Bournemouth; as we passed Southampton, we could see the 'Queen Mary' liner in dock. To get from Bournemouth to Poole we took a Hants & Dorset double decker, local service bus. During my parents first encounter with Poole just before the War, they had made friends with a couple slightly older but who never had children. By 1947, the couple had moved to a typical Dorset thatched cottage in the village of Lytchett Matravers, to the west of Poole; the cottage had a large garden and an old well where the butter and milk was lowered in a bucket to keep it cool in the summertime (fridges were not a standard household feature in those days). We made many memorable day trips to places like Swanage, Wimbourne, Chapman's Pool, Corfe Castle and the Blue Pool, and our mode of transport was an 'S' type sports Jaguar. At the end of a very hot day at Lulworth Cove rounded off with lobster salad (adults only! - not for me such a luxury) in a local restaurant, we ventured home, up a rough track from the Cove and succumbed to the motorists dread – a puncture and no spare tyre! However, we resolved our plight by removing the inner tube and stuffing the tyre with grass and harvested straw, this improvisation was probably a make shift technique my father learned in the army; I am pleased to recall it got us safely back to the cottage that evening so that we could continue the enjoyable holiday before returning back to Hastings.

This holiday in Dorset, my birth county, with such glorious weather after the hard winter, really set family life on a more optimistic course than that of the recent war and immediate post war years of uncertainty. For me in particular, it was the end of my first two years at primary school during which time I had contracted rather severely, nearly all the childhood ailments except scarlet fever; I had a dangerous attack of whooping cough which put me back in a pram at the age of 5 – thank goodness there is now a vaccine for this and several of the other childhood diseases. These were also still the days when tuberculosis (TB) was common, my mother's eldest sister succumbed to this terrible disease and died in 1938 leaving two children, my eldest first cousins, a boy and a girl. Then in 1942, my father's eldest brother, married with no children, also died of TB – this uncle was my first memory in life, at the age of 2. There were children my age right through schooling into the 1950's who had had TB and recovered, or had been afflicted with that other dreadful disease, polio myelitis leaving children with deformed or weak limbs supported by iron frames – these were not uncommon sights. Medical science producing antibiotics and ever more vaccines in the last 60 years, has done wonders in virtually eliminating these afflictions and improving our health generally, world wide.

Father in Military Police uniform (a Redcap).

Note black disc badge on right arm signifying he was in the Berlin area in 1945 -'46

Father on a BSA motorcycle passing through northern France (Lille)

en route to his destiny Berlin.

The Reichstag, Berlin.

August 1945

The Brandenberg Gate, Berlin.

August 1945

3. Ancestors in the Weald

Back to Hastings and back to school, 1947 ended with a sad family loss, my grandmother Booth, my father's mother died age 70 of pneumonia at the Buchanan hospital (now demolished and replaced by housing), a couple of weeks before Christmas. In her later years during the War, grandmother Booth and grandfather Booth were 'living in' caretakers at Park View clinic, a Victorian house opposite the Park Gates at Bohemia just down the road from Park Road Methodist Church. I can remember collecting my free government allocation of Virol, orange juice and cod liver oil from the clinic to help build up my young, thin body, typical of many war time children, although I was not undernourished. Before Park view, my grandparents Booth had lived at Bexhill Road St. Leonards - on - Sea where my father was born in 1914, and then to Landsview Terrace on The Ridge.

Grandfather Booth used to breed Dutch rabbits in hutches at the side of the clinic and win cups at shows. His early years were spent at Sandhurst, Kent ('hurst' - settlement on a wooded hill), a village deeper into the Weald, where he was born, his father William was a humble agricultural labourer, his mother Sarah Barnes was from another Sandhurst family. When my grandfather Booth was in his early 20's at the end of the 19th century, having had experience of riding horses 'bare back' delivering medicines for the village doctor, he volunteered for military service with the Prince of Wales 12th Lancers. This opportunity to ride horses and take him out of his small Kentish community, took him to South Africa to fight in the Boer War. It also gave him the privilege to be present on horse back in full uniform along the route in London that Queen Victoria took for her Diamond Jubilee celebrations in 1897. These experiences would have made a great impact on the mind of a young man of humble stock from a country village. Unfortunately, an elder brother George (my great uncle), was killed fighting with the 1st/5th South Lancashire Regiment on the Somme in 1916 in the 1st World War at the age of 40.

Grandmother Booth was also born in Sandhurst, Kent but into the Newman family of slightly higher village status, being master butchers. The family home and shop were off the Back Road from the village green. With both the Boer War ended and the reign of Queen Victoria with her death at the beginning of the 20th century, grandfather and grandmother Booth were married at St. Nicholas Church, Sandhurst in 1903 and moved to Hastings.

The death of grandmother Booth was the first death of one of my grandparents. Her funeral was at St. Nicholas Church, Sandhurst and she is buried in the churchyard, as is grandfather Booth who died 16 years later at the age of 85. Grandmother's grave became a focus for an annual excursion to Sandhurst usually on Easter Monday in the immediate years after her death. We used to take the no. 84 Maidstone & District double decker bus (better views from the top deck than from a car) from Wellington Square, Hastings (buses going into the country areas used to park on the tarmac below the grassed area of the square); we eventually got off at Sandhurst cross roads and made the short walk along the lane to the church.

Sandhurst churchyard is a most tranquil spot on a high hill in the Weald with views to the south across the Rother valley, near Bodiam Castle into East Sussex; Fairlight church can be seen on the hills above the Wealden shore, about 16 miles away. To the west rise some of the highest hills of the Weald beyond Brightling Needle and to the north and east scanning left to right is the flatter landscape beyond Tenterden engaging the Rother valley as it fans out into the Romney Marsh with the North Downs in the far distance. In the mid-distance in East Sussex, is an extensive wooded area within which at Northiam, is the well-known Great Dixter house with its wonderful gardens established by

Christopher Lloyd (Christo), writer of garden books who died in 2006 age 85. It is worth commenting that Great Dixter was once a 15th century manor house purchased by Christopher Lloyd's father Nathaniel Lloyd in 1910, and he together with the fashionable Edwardian architect Edwin Lutyens rebuilt the house and designed the lay out of the garden. I can recall taking another bus with my parents and sister to Northiam in about 1951 and making the short walk to Great Dixter., whereupon Christo's mother Daisy sitting with her dog in the timbered porch, took our entrance fee. Christo, then a young man of 30 with his distinctive crisp curly hair, was proud to show us and a group around the house and the beautiful garden   I shall never forget the distinct, timeless, aromatic odour of wax polish which was preserving the numerous pieces of antique furniture dispersed among the many rooms in the old house. In the 1930's, there was a chauffeur at Great Dixter called Booth, he could well have been a relative of mine with so many of my family living in the area.

It is perhaps not surprising that the authoress Patience Strong, writer of short stories and poems concerned with the spiritual aspect of life, should be buried in St Nicholas churchyard with its atmosphere of tranquility, in fact, in the same row as Patience Strong's grave, is the grave of our eldest daughter Amanda Jane who sadly died of leukaemia at the age of 4 in 1972.   This poignant event and the burial of my grandparents and indeed great and great, great grandparents and many descendents in this churchyard, is an extra reason for continuing at least an annual pilgrimage to this place and to absorb the splendid scenery bringing back many memories of earlier lives.

Back to the days following my grandmother Booth's burial at Sandhurst, and the subsequent annual visit to the churchyard at Easter, I recall my parents and I, and later my sister Rosalind taking a picnic lunch at the edge of the field through a swing gate on the south side of the churchyard. On one occasion high in the rotten trunk of an ash tree by the swing gate, was a 'sleeping' tawny owl looking down on us with a suspicious eye! Behind us as we sat looking west across a field with spring lambs approaching their mothers with pleading bleets, seeking their milky lunch, was a long narrow copse with its floor carpeted with bluebells, primroses and wood anemones, so typically a Wealden habitat – what better exposure could one have of the atmosphere of spring, miles away from any significant urban development and no sound of traffic?

The afternoon was often taken up with visiting great aunts and uncles and father's cousins living in Sandhurst or in the neighbouring village of Hawkhurst. One of these relatives was the oldest relative I can remember, great, great uncle Alfred Barnes, my grandfather Booth's uncle in his late 80's in the late 1940's, and therefore born in the 1860's. The image I recall of uncle Alfred was an old man with long white hair and beard resembling Charles Darwin that great biologist who wrote the 'Origin of Species' about 90 years earlier, but my uncle was a much humbler man sitting in the corner of a cottage by an old kitchen range in Sponden Lane, Sandhurst being looked after by his niece, my great aunt Polly, my grandfather Booth's sister. Uncle Alfred Barnes had been a Baptist lay preacher, a surname associated with a Dorset cleric William Barnes known for his poems written in Dorset dialect. It is by coincidence that I had three great grandparents with namesake surnames associated with the church, the others being William Booth founder of the Salvation Army as mentioned earlier, and mine and my father's Christian name as well, then there is my grandmother of the Sandhurst butcher family with the name of Newman; a John Henry Newman (now canonized as a Saint), was an Anglican priest before conversion to becoming a Catholic cardinal – all these clerics were men of the 19th century, living in the same period as my grandparents generation.

Before we leave Sandhurst, there was one walk we did from Sandhurst churchyard after we had, had our picnic in the field to the south. We continued down the footpath to the bottom of the field where we turned right along a dusty track by Old Place. From here our walk took us back on to the main road to Hastings via Bodiam. Turning left along this road with very little traffic in those days, we walked the mile and a half to Bodiam. About half way along the road in a valley, is the Kent Ditch, a small stream on the boundary between Kent and East Sussex. To the right of the road by the stream was a house with a disused water mill known as Bodiam Mill, indicated by the rusting wheel collapsing into the stream and becoming overgrown with waterside plants such as the great willowherb. Once again, my emotional response to this decaying metal carcass, like that of the twisted rusty metal remains of a 'doodlebug' I saw a few years earlier, was that even inanimate, artefacts of human origin, have a limited life span.

We continued our walk up the hill and down the other side into Bodiam, it was now mid - afternoon giving us time to visit the well-preserved medieval castle built in the 14th century for Sir Edward Dalingridge as a defense against the French who could attack up the Rother valley from the sea; they never did, leaving the castle in good condition to be used today for film sets. What fascinated me here apart from my interest in old places, was the extensive deep moat completely surrounding the castle which overflows into the River Rother; at one time there was a wharf from the river to the castle. But the real fascination was the presence of the large carp in the moat, cruising under the surface, one moment exposed for all to see, the.next concealed by the large water lily pads. These fish may have been here for centuries, once food for the inhabitants of the castle. After our stroll round the castle, there was one of those village tea rooms nearby to revive us for our journey home back on the no. 84 bus, and time to reflect on such a rewarding family outing.

41

My following poem endeavours to emphasize the emotional response to the scent of flowers in a country lane, or garden, which release distant and nostalgic memories:

'Honeysuckle'

Fanfares and duets of golden floral trumpets
Blasting forth notes of nature's most exquisite perfume
To reach a crescendo on a warm spring evening.

Such music to the nose penetrating to the depths of long
Stored memories – parent's garden, first love in a Sussex lane.

Just a few molecules of scent, a hint of cloves draped
With lilies, so little to transpose the here and now conciousness
To the virtual reality of a consuming memory.

Archetypal reflections of the mysterious East,
Wherever that might be?

From there to here, and back again,
A continuum bridging the past with the present,
The essence of life, needing only the essence of a flower.

View looking NE to St. Nicholas Church, Sandhurst, Kent.

Picnics were taken by the hedgerow and footpath on the right.

(in recent years, the pastureland has been ploughed for arable crops).

View looking SW from St. Nicholas Church, Sandhurst, Kent.

'Old Place' is mid-view on the left and the Rother Valley near Bodiam Castle,

to the High Weald at Brightling in the far distance on the right.

4. Family Walks from the Doorstep

My father never owned a car, the only motorized vehicle he had was the BSA motor bike in the War. This meant that my parents and I, and later my sister Rosalind and brother Clive were dependent upon buses and trains for journeys longer than those we would normally walk. Already I have described the walk to Pett Level as a seaside excursion, but there were other favourite jaunts my parents used to take the family on, sometimes again a combination of walking and a bus ride. Hastings itself had, and still has, many interesting walks to offer and the fact that the town and 1066 is remembered as an historical event by just about everyone schooled in Britain, the area also has much to offer to those interested in local history and natural history.

An important introduction to these cultural topics was being taken to the Hastings Museum at John's Place off Cambridge Road and seeing dinosaur displays (always an appeal to young children) including footprint casts of the plant eating version of T. rex, the Iguanodon retrieved from the sandstone cliff falls at Fairlight – another revelation of the Wealden shore. (Many years later, I too found similar footprint casts associated with ripple casts on a large slab of sandstone on the beach at Fairlight. This find was confirmed by the curator of the museum John Manwaring Baines FSA and is recorded in a photograph being admired by our daughter Rebecca).

A destination of a different character, was being taken by my father to King's Road in St. Leonards to see the Christmas illuminations. It was only a few years after the War and because it was an evening event after dark, it was a magical experience for me, particularly having a late night out with just my father. We did not have a Christmas tree with lights, so the shopping area of Kings Road crisscrossed with strands of colourful lights was an enthralling event. But the 'icing on the cake' at the end of the evening was calling into a small cafe on the sea front and father buying me a snack of Spam fritters – my favourite! How could I forget this evening? The other late evening during the Christmas period full of magical exposure, was being taken to a pantomime at the White Rock Pavilion – the experience of going home after the pantomime on the last bus, in itself seemed a dream-like event to a young child.

A favourite family walk, was to walk from Hoad's Wood Road towards the town and over the West Hill to the Old Town. This walk led us up and down steps and along narrow passages known locally as 'twittens' connecting one road with another. In the Old Town we would browse around the many second hand and antique shops where in the early years after the War, items costing a few shillings could be found; my father with always an eye and emotional sensitivity for images of the past, was to start his small collection to give no.18 a cottage like atmosphere. The largest item father bought was an 18th century cottage grandfather clock made in Surrey with just the hour hand and quarter of an hour divisions on the face instead of the usual five on a two handed clock. The clock cost only £5 and was finished with a dark black stain.

My father soon got to work on the clock after work in the evenings, unshackled from his stiff shop suit, collar and tie and with an old striped shirt, sleeves rolled up, he started stripping off the horrible stain with a chemical stripper and metal scraper over newspapers covering the dining room table. The case of the clock was in two parts, the main body for the ropes, weight and pendulum, and the removable hood which covered the main mechanism and face. Once all the stain had been painstakingly removed, there was exposed a beautiful light oak wood. The final stage in the restoration of this time piece was to rub a mixture of turpentine and bees wax into the wood, giving a light gloss to the natural colour of the oak; a new rope was fitted to the pulleys and weight system, and the clock started to tick in the corner of the dining room, plus the loud strike every hour for the next 60 years, (I can still hear that subdued one second tick and harsh ring of the strike as a nostalgic memory). Often walks to the Old Town would end with the purchase from a fish stall at the Fish Market of bloaters or kippers for high tea, or for a real treat, some fresh sweet scallops from Rye Bay which my mother would braise in milk, butter and bread crumbs – scrumptious!

Before we leave the Old Town, opposite St Clement's Church on the High Street there used to be a pet shop, a venue where all children loved to peer through the windows on the road frontage and the dark alley way at the side leading to Winding Street. On the other side of the glass were enduring young kittens and puppies, guinea pigs and rabbits, and sometimes less cuddly creatures such as tortoises. My 9th birthday was coming up and I wanted a guinea pig as a present. My father and I acquired an old orange box from the grocers and with hinges, screws and wire netting converted the fruit box into a cosy hutch – I painted the door yellow with a maroon floral design, rather like a gypsy caravan! Now what did the pet shop have to put into this hutch for my birthday? There peering through the window of the shop, tucked away in the corner was a black and tan, adult, female guinea pig which caught my eye. After my father paid the fee, into a cardboard box went this little glossy and smooth coated animal, to put in a new purpose built home. Birthday over, a few days later when I went to feed 'Sally' my new pet, there were three guinea pigs – small, new born, a ginger one and the other like Mum; I had got three for the price of one. This was a commercial gain years before the supermarkets took up this procedure for increasing their profits, but never again did I have such luck with a business transaction. Our black and white cat 'Whisky' (named after a brand of the alcoholic drink), just looked on and grinned at the prospect of three guinea pigs escaping from this intrusive box in his territory!

Another local area for walks was covering different areas of Alexandra Park from the lakes, lawns, tennis courts and rose beds, to the wooded areas including the magnificent rhododendrons of the Shornden reservoir valley and the trickling stream through the upper valley of the Park known as Old Roar Gill. After heavy rain, the small stream in Old Roar valley became swollen enough to produce a waterfall at the end of the gill – this was 'Old Roar'! This water keeps the Buckshole reservoir topped up before it joins water flowing from the Shornden valley and Ore valley to form the main stream flowing through the length of the Park and was called the Priory stream running out to sea through what is now the 'new' town of Hastings. Before the town was developed in the late 18th and 19th centuries, particularly with the coming of the railway, the area was known as Priory meadows because of the nearby old priory situated near the present main post office (today the name is retained as the new shopping centre on the site of the once well-known Sussex cricket ground). The interesting landscape feature of small ravines, glens and valleys connecting the former to the latter with an increase in the water out flow over a relatively short mileage, is a distinctive feature of the drainage of the Weald towards the coast as referred to earlier between Pett Level and Rye.

I cannot leave the memories of Alexandra Park without mentioning three aspects which impressed a child's mind. The first was walking with my parents up Upper Park Road to the south of the Shornden reservoir, late on a cold October afternoon and kicking sweet chestnut cases (looking like miniature hedgehogs), with stout, black, school boy shoes to expose those mahogany coloured chestnuts which you eat, not the Horse chestnuts of conker fame. The acid soil of the Weald and higher average temperatures of Sussex support the growth of the sweet chestnut tree, whereas the Horse chestnut tree is found more widely in Britain; it is the acid condition of the soil in Alexandra Park and in the surrounding countryside which also supports the presence of rhododendrons. A pocket full of fat sweet chestnuts would be taken home on a Sunday afternoon and roasted over an open fire after crumpets for tea; the toasting aroma and glow of the log fire was an introduction to approaching winter. Near to Upper Park Road on the steep wooded slopes above the stream and rose garden in the Park, there were large grassy mounds running vertically up the slope, they were called 'giants graves', why, I am not sure, perhaps they were left over from the days when hop gardens were here before the Park. Above these mounds was a track separating the Shornden valley from the main Park. We had to cross the track before going down some steps to the pumping station. On one occasion our route across the track was interrupted by thousands of tiny frogs, half an inch long migrating out of Harmer's ponds downstream from the Shornden reservoir; how could we avoid treading on these innocent creatures? Somehow we did.

Walking further up the Park beyond the rose garden brought us to the pumping station situated down the valley from Buckshole reservoir and Dr MaCabes chalybeate spring (rich in iron and sulphur, available to drink with cupped hands, but tasted like blood!) This pumping station was steam operated and often when returning home on a Sunday morning from Park Road Methodist Church (my father was a Methodist and my mother Anglican), the pumping station would be pumping water from the reservoir with a regular expulsion of steam from a pipe high up on the outer wall sounding like a steam train going nowhere - fascinating to a child; on one occasion we had the opportunity to go through the green 'stable' type doors into the building and see the big wheel and associated engineering operating the pump. Some years ago the need for water arising from the Buckshole reservoir for the 'new' town of Hastings, was diminished with the opening of the extensive Bewl Water reservoir near Lamberhurst supplying water; this resulted in the closure and demolition of the pumping station in Alexandra Park. Another memory of the Park at this stage of my life, was sitting in deck chairs with my parents on a Sunday afternoon and listening to a band playing old favourites like 'In a Monastery Garden' in the permanent band stand situated on the lawn area at the centre of the Park; welcomed refreshments were readily available in the nearby tea room particularly on a hot summer afternoon.

My father liked English tea rooms and I have mentioned the tea room enshrouded in reeds and willow trees at Pett Level. Another favourite walk which ended up at a tea room was for my parents and I to re-trace the walk my mother, grandparents James and I did in the War years, this was to set off down Stonestile Lane. Now with my father as the motivator, thrilled to be back home with his family, we walked further on to Westfield, perhaps stopping for a drink at the Plough (this was my first acquaintance with the 'Bottle and Jug', an annex in public houses where children were allowed to collect a non-alcoholic drink and with an adult, take alcoholic drink such as beer to the working men on a farm etc.). From here we walked on another 3 miles to Sedlescombe, and during this last part of the journey we would have a picnic lunch somewhere off road in a field (today, a pioneering vineyard operated by Carr Taylor exists just off the lane near Westfield). This lane like Stonestile Lane also had primroses cascading down its banks in spring, but by summer the banks became dry and the plants parched, it was here as you walked by that the common lizard basking in the sun would suddenly scuttle away causing the dry leaves from the previous autumn leaf fall to crackle and give away the presence of this defensive creature.

By mid-afternoon we would reach Sedlescombe facing up hill to the long village green with attractive period houses and cottages, lining the two roads each either side of the green; some of the buildings were timber framed, others red brick with hanging tiles on the walls of the first floors – all typically Sussex, were a common architectural feature. We had a choice of three tea rooms, all different in their location. The first one we would come to from Westfield, was the Tythe Barn on the right just past the stone bridge on the main road breaching the River Brede which was quite small and fast flowing at this point on its journey down the valley to meet the River Rother at Rye; the Tythe Barn was a timbered building and quaint, with an owl as a sign outside. Almost opposite was the Waterfall Tea Gardens reached after a short walk by the river. As the name implies these tea gardens had the River Brede flowing through them which cascaded down a small waterfall before entering a large pool, this was a cool spot to relax with a cup of tea and cake under the trees surrounding the pool. I later recorded this tranquil site in about 1956 as a black and white photograph taken on my mother's old Kodak Brownie box camera which I then transposed to an oil painting. At the top end of Sedlescombe was a large building called the Brickwall Hotel which was open to non residents, from here you got a good view down the length of the village. We did not walk back to Hastings, too late in the day, so we caught a Maidstone & District bus back to town, the same service that took us further in land to Sandhurst.

Other tea rooms we visited after a bus journey and walking, were to Battle, Catsfield, Northiam and Rye. My father always sought out the tea rooms with character i.e. those with beams and open fire places and distinctive smell of wax polished furniture, in short an 'old world' atmosphere. It must have been these experiences which added to my interest in vernacular history. Such was the pleasure of simple leisure in the 1940's and 1950's. Our legs and affordable bus fares took us out into the Wealden countryside to absorb its timeless heritage, preceding and following that notable date, 1066. Today people flash through the same landscape in their cars but do they really experience this in the same way as we did 50 years ago? I am not sure, but there are not the same number of tea rooms around today to sit in and reflect on the day's outing, even public houses are disappearing and the exhilaration experienced by a walk in the countryside is often now limited to rambling clubs and sponsored walks.

It was during the time that these family excursions to the countryside occurred, that my father in 1948 was very fortunate to be offered the manager's post at Hepworth's retail tailor's shop in Queen's Road, Hastings; this opportunity enabled my father to get back to the employment which he had left behind in Poole at the beginning of the War and continue his position in Hastings until he retired in the 1970's. I am sure my father's employment in retail tailoring suited his personality, he liked to dress well. Earlier in his youth he was proud to be the flag bearer in the Boys Brigade based at Park Road Methodist Church, wearing the distinctive navy and white trimmed uniform with cap. Likewise during the War, father always looked smart and alert in military uniform. Concerned to have a respectable appearance in public without being ostentatious and a sense of duty in all that he did, were attributes instilled in my father at a young age through his father's Victorian upbringing and attendance at the Methodist church.

Among father's many customers was Tom Cookson, my later maths and form master at the Grammar School and husband of the authoress Catherine Cookson. A regular purchase was the typical Harris tweed jacket worn by schoolmasters, so durable and long lasting which Tom said to my father, *"I always keep the jackets after the class room days for gardening !"* Didn't we all do that? So normal, but today people like Tom with a good income, might buy 'special' gardening clothes, but they would not be like Tom, he was down to earth to the end even when he no longer needed to be a schoolmaster because of his wife's income. Incidently, Tom and Catherine were very enthusiastic gardeners, a relaxation from their demanding professions; they had landscaped the Hurst and even more so their second home in St. Helen's Wood, 'Loreto' with

51

terraces and a natural woodland area including Wealden oak trees.

Rebecca with the three-toed, foot print cast of an Iguanodon

at Fairlight Cove in 1975.

The Waterfall Tea Gardens, Sedlescombe.

(photograph of original oil painting by the author)

View of Rye Town Centre

from the tower of St. Mary's Church in about 1960.

Tom Cookson wearing his Hepworth's,

Harris tweed (schoolmaster's) jacket.

© Sarah Sables

Sketch Map of Hoad's Wood in the 1950's

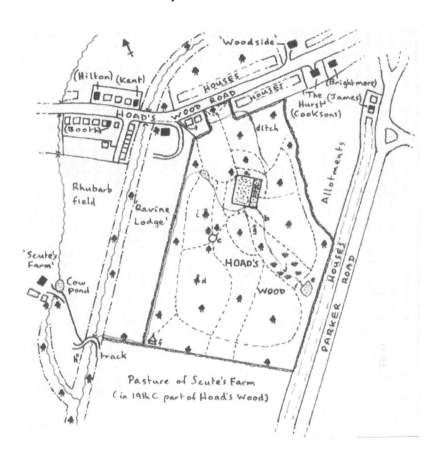

Key: --------------------- footpaths   boundary of ravines

(a) old tennis court; (b) small stream for 'Pooh' sticks; (c) 'clearing'; (d) sparrow hawk's nest in fir tree;

(e) duck pond with palmate newts; (f) 'corner camp'; (g) site of long tailed tit's nest; (h) badger's sett;

(i) wood pigeon's nest; (j) the 'swamps'; (k) night camp area

55

5. The Enchanted Wood

I suppose it was when I was about 7 or 8 years old that I was allowed to venture forth from home 'to go out to play' after school, at weekends and during school holidays without being accompanied by my parents. I had of course travelled to and from St. Andrew's school on my own before this age because there was a direct bus to town caught from the Dorset Laundry on Elphinstone Road at the junction with Hoad's Wood Road. I would alight at the railway bridge at the top of Queen's Road, followed by a short walk to the school. The bus stop for the return journey was by the Clock House on Queen's Road, this off licence sold all types of drinks and Smith's crisps with the inherent blue bag of salt for a one or two pence, a treat I indulged while waiting for the bus, (one thing has not changed, our grand children do this today, but the menu is more diverse). Once a week, I would ascend the steep flight of steps beside the school at the bottom of Nelson Road, only a couple of hundred yards from the Grammar School I was later to attend; a bus stop near the top of the steps took me to Parker Road for tea with my mother and grandparents James.

But returning to 'out to play', where and who with? Hoad's Wood Road in the late 1940's was still an unadopted, rough surfaced road in suburbia, but more in the countryside than the town. You could walk from the road with its cinder paths straight into Hoad's Wood, visible up the road from our house; oak trees at the entrance heralded a predominantly deciduous wood with a handful of pine trees typical of a Wealden wood. Further up the road on the left was another wood which led to a ravine with a small stream which was part of the catchment for the Priory stream in Alexandra Park; soon after the War this wood was cut down for a housing development, the only indicator that a wood was nearby was the Victorian house 'Woodside' just down the road and on the other side from the Cooksons at 'The Hurst'. Hoad's Wood itself remained until around 1960 when it too was replaced by housing and a new road Lindley Drive. However, before this obliteration of a natural habitat on one's doorstep, I was fortunate together with other boys and girls in Hoad's Wood Road and Parker Road to have this wood to play in and receive my unofficial education in natural history.

I had one friend in particular who used to come to our house to play before I started school in 1945, this was Barry who was 15 months older than me. Barry lived with his parents, an older brother John, a younger brother Paul and a younger sister Pat (a year younger than me); this family named Kent were in a small detached house diagonally opposite from my parents house. The children of the Kent family were like brothers and sister to me because I had to wait until I was 9 before my sister Rosalind was born and another 7 years before my brother Clive arrived – by this time I was 16 and studying for my 'O' levels.

From the immediate post War years until our mid teens, my contemporaries including Barry and his brothers and sister had the opportunity to play in Hoad's Wood where we would recapitulate some aspects of our ancestral human behaviour by exploring, building camps with the splayed branches of hazel trees for the walls and ferns for the floors, and even having mock 'tribal' battles with children who lived on the other side of Hoad's Wood in Parker Road whose back gardens bordered the wood. We were in essence reflecting the theme of William Golding's novel 'Lord of the Flies' where children organize their own society on an island divorced from adult influences, but of course we were not living in this extreme situation, we were not separated from adult influences. Our weapons, never seriously used, were bows and arrows made from the straight hazel growths in the wood and dust bin lids were our shields; thankfully no one was hurt and we all returned to our respective road – home territories to meet another day in the wood, this time as friends. We did not realize as innocent children that we were acting out the primitive instincts of aggression related to the possession of territory expressed by adults throughout the world which, sadly, Darwinian evolution has not yet progressed us too far from animals. I can remember my mother making me a Red Indian chief's head dress from our chickens' wing feathers fixed into curtain tape. How important I must have felt with this symbol of leadership on my head during our mock battles influenced by the predominant exposure to cowboy and Indian films seen at the cinema, notably, at the ABC minors at the Ritz in town on a Saturday morning. However, subconciously, cowboys and Indians was not the only source of tribal aggression we were exposed to, we had just been growing up through a world war and now the Korean war was underway. Thankfully, these scars of civilisation were not going to quench my enthusiasm for learning about the natural world and the more positive endeavours of mankind as the years went by.

Hoad's Wood began to play its part in stimulating my appetite for natural history. By the age of 10 the appearance, song, type of nest and colour of eggs of several of our common birds were familiar to me. My eldest cousin Gwen who was 10 years older than me and at our house on holiday, became aware of my interest in birds particularly after I showed her a thrush's nest containing pale blue eggs and dark spots at one end, in a hedgerow; before Gwen left she bought me the 1950's edition of the Observer's Book of British Birds, one of only eleven Observer's titles produced at that time. This book was the bible for birds to me and I still have it, well thumbed; all the images and descriptions of the birds and their habitats are well engraved in my brain. I shall never forget the finding of my first long tailed tit's nest in the depths of Hoad's Wood, suspended in a tangle of small twigs by spiders' webs like a hammock; the body of the nest was impregnated with moss and the whole lined with soft feathers and containing a large clutch of the smallest of white eggs. It is a wonder of nature how this small nest can accommodate the whole family which is due to its expanding structure arising from the plasticity of the spiders' webs.

Climbing trees was a preoccupation of Barry and I, either hazel to gather the nuts in the autumn, or the much larger 100 year old oak trees to get a bird's-eye view of the smaller trees and ground flora below; sometimes it was hiding from other children who were not aware of our presence above them! Today I get vertigo just thinking about this activity as we saddled the rough oak boughs, perhaps 20-30 feet up. A hawthorn tree on one occasion contained a wood pigeon's nest at its summit. For weeks I would climb this tree to see when the eggs were laid and the two young hatch on the thin layer of twigs, such a precarious home. At this time, I had become aware of the attraction of dove cotes in old gardens such as those where we made our family excursions into the countryside. Could I take these young pigeons away from their nest to a 'better' home, a dove cote in my parents garden? Sheer fascination with this prospect. However, this was not to be, parents would not have approved and the young innocent pigeons were either taken by a magpie or other bird of prey such as a sparrow hawk which was common before the days of over use of chlorinated pesticides, (these contaminated the food chain for birds of prey which then produced soft shelled eggs which did not survive). Anyway, young wood pigeons are unlikely to have taken to a dove cote and become domesticated.

One way of impressing the appearance of birds' eggs on the mind, was to collect them, fortunately now an illegal action. Over 50 years ago it was considered acceptable to take just one egg from a clutch, pierce each end with a pin and blow very gently through the hole at the wide end of the egg, this art resulted in evacuating the egg shell of its albuminous contents, but if addled or with an embryo this was not a pleasant experience. A tray of colourful birds' eggs was a collector's appeal, but today this is history for a museum collection.

I was drawn to the attention of the sparrow hawk on two other occasions. The first was while my parents and I were having our lunch, suddenly there was a disturbance on the small lawn outside the dining room window as a sparrow hawk plummeted down on one of the starlings which regularly nested in the eaves above my bedroom window above the dining room; needless to say the hawk 'joined us' in its midday meal. The second encounter was after climbing up a tall Scots pine tree near 'the clearing' in Hoad's Wood. At the top of this tree, straight and vertical as a telegraph pole with only broken off branches leaving stumps to act as foot holds to climb the tree, I was face to face with a sparrow hawk's nest containing two eggs. Soon I was to return with a friend's modern plastic camera and I took my first photograph, it was of the sparrow hawk's nest, I was 13; fortunately the parent birds did not return to the nest during my presence to mock me whereupon I might have lost my grip on the tree with very serious consequences!

Another natural history opportunity provided by Hoad's Wood was caterpillar beating. Barry and I would borrow our fathers' discarded black umbrellas, open them upside down under leafy branches and beat the branches with a stick, it was revealing, the numbers and diversity of caterpillars and other entomological specimens that fell into the umbrellas; we endeavoured to identify some of the creatures but it was the thrill of dislodging this Aladdin's cave of insect life that was important.

Other creatures collected from the woods were at dusk with the aid of a hand torch, held in stout leather gloves, because we were hunting for hedgehogs. We used to listen for their rustling movements in the leaves and then home in on the source of the sound with our torches, the hedgehogs were revealed defensively rolled into a ball and we would gently pick them up in our gloves and take them home. Barry and I only kept these temporary pets for a day or so to watch them feeding on the worms and scraps from the kitchen we provided before we returned them back to the same area of the wood where they were captured.

At the top of Hoad's Wood adjacent to one of the back gardens of Parker Road, was a small shallow pond topped up by one of the many springs oozing from the Wealden clay soil. This pond we called the duck pond, although I do not recall seeing any ducks on it, but beneath its surface a few inches below on the muddy bottom there were numerous palmated newts, either stationary absorbing the warm sun's rays as they penetrated through the overhanging trees into the water, or making sudden movements as they were disturbed by our presence; they are called palmated newts because the males have webbed hind feet. I have never seen before, or since so many newts in one place. The wood sloped gently south west from the duck pond and the ground was water logged, we called it the 'swamps' and the mud was nearly to the top of our Wellington boots. Here growing in abundance was the pendulous sedge, *Carex pendula*. (This plant has followed me through my life being first transplanted to my parents garden in Hoad's Wood Road and then to our present garden in Cambridgeshire).

Returning to my childhood and the hours spent in Hoad's Wood. One evening when I was about 12 years old, a group of boys including me, decided to camp out overnight in late spring. We did not have proper tents so we improvised with old sheets and rain coats and supporting sticks from the hazel in the wood. My tent had my father's war time groundsheet put to good use again to keep the damp away from my body in my make shift bed. The 'tents' were assembled on the top of a grassy bank adjacent to the old tennis court in the middle of the wood; this was always our assembly point for social gatherings. All I can remember of that night was the hard ground and almost continuous song of a nightingale in the trees above us from dusk to dawn, quite a unique experience and I suppose worth missing a night's sleep, which I did. Opposite the 'camp site' where you entered the tennis court from a woodland path leading back to the entrance of the wood in Hoad's Wood Road, there was a large old oak tree and under this I saw my first bee orchid with its flower looking as its name suggests, like a happy bee on a summer flower.

At the south end of Hoad's Wood we emerged from the wood through a number of gaps in the hedge above a small ditch, into the meadows of Scute's Farm. Incidently the hedge row above the ditch was predominantly holly and the leaf fall over decades had produced a rich leaf mould which I gathered in a sack and transported home on a go-cart. Scute's Farm accessed by a track from Elphinstone Road, was operated by a Welshman, Mr Nash and his wife, they had two grown up daughters, one I recall was a nurse. The farm had six fields of natural pasture land for 12 dairy cows to graze and the fields were alive with grass hoppers and butterflies circulating among the diverse species of wild flowers, (an increasingly less common sight today with the use of pesticides and herbicides). In addition there were two fields devoted to rhubarb, one of which was close to my parents' house, separated only by a bungalow, the other abutted on to the Dorset Laundry and Elphintone Road. The whole farmland was divided by two wooded ravines, each with a stream, one through the farmyard forming a pond where the cows could drink, the other running from the grounds of Ravine Lodge, another Victorian house in Hoad's Wood Road. These water courses merged and eventually flowed into the Ore valley and on into the stream in Alexandra Park.

Although Scute's Farm was private land with no public footpaths, we used to explore the area and Mr Nash was amenable to our presence. This exploring was often more organized by leaving a message for a 'search party' on a piece of paper left by a 'hiding party', in the bark of a tree known to everybody playing the game. The message might say "next clue on the fence post at the beginning of the farm track in the ravine", and so on, a chain of clues was followed until the 'search party' found the 'hiding party' near the last clue – perhaps under the tall sticks of rhubarb, some being nibbled as false refreshment and then discarded with wincing faces due to the sourness of the fruit! The one time rhubarb sticks were not discarded was during an Easter school holiday when I picked rhubarb for Mr Nash to earn a few extra shillings.

I cannot leave Scute's Farm without recalling the wonderful encounter with badgers. It was in the late 1950's, the last few years of the farm's existence and Hoad's Wood too before the developers moved in, that a badger's sett became established in one of the ravines on the farm near a track joining two meadows, (today this part of the ravine still exists next to the children's play area opposite the junction of Wilmington Road, once a cul-de-sac of Hoad's Wood Road and Linley Drive). On a warm summer's evening, my friend Barry and I would sit on old stools with Mrs Nash and watch the badgers emerge from the sett a few feet away, cautiously, first parents and then young trusting our presence, emerged to feast on the milk and bread we offered them. Sadly, one day, the the adult male was found dead in Hoad's Wood and I retrieved its skull to add to my collection of animal skulls which I retained to improve my knowledge of anatomy until I went to university.

One final recollection of childhood activity in Hoad's Wood, was racing Pooh sticks, that most Wealden of activities as epitomized in A. A. Milne' stories centred around Ashdown Forest in north Sussex. Hoad's Wood as implicated earlier, was riddled with small streams which were enhanced after heavy rain. Barry and I would select tiny light weight sticks, about a couple of inches long and the best for floating would be elder twigs or dried out stems of umbelliferous plants. We would place the sticks parallel to start their competitive journey, in a stream flowing down through the wood and keep the sticks moving with a long stick until one of the sticks reached a defined destination and declared the winner. There must be a gene for this behaviour because Barry and I not being familiar with the details of the Winnie the Pooh stories at that time, did not call them Pooh sticks.

Adjacent to Hoad's Wood, was a garden in Hoad's Wood Road through which a small stream ran out from the wood., the garden belonged to the Clark's and they had two sons, the eldest being Michael. contemporary in age to Barry and I. Somehow we managed to persuade Michael's father to allow us to build a dam round the stream to form a pond, and this we did quite successfully using the water retaining clay soil from the garden. The pond was quite large probably about 8 feet wide, 12 feet long and a foot deep. Barry and I soon acquired some water weeds and snails from the various ponds we had discovered, and best of all we had a haven for some of the freshwater fish we caught on our fishing trips and managed to keep them alive until we got home; these were roach, rudd and tench. In the ravine next to Barry's house, there was another small stream (which eventually was one of the water courses which passed through the land of Scute's Farm); here we built another dam and placed weed, snails and common newts in another, but smaller pond to observe the aquatic life until the stream swelled after heavy rain and washed our 'aquarium' away!

Sparrow hawk's nest at the top of a Scots pine tree

in Hoad's Wood in June 1953.

(the author climbed the tree to take the photograph

with a 'modern' plastic Kodak camera)

Palmated newts in the 'duck pond' surrounded by

the pendulous sedge *Carex pendula* at Hoad's Wood.

Left: male; Right: female

6. St. Helen's – Woods, Churches and back Home

St. Helen's Wood was the other wood we explored as children, about a mile from Hoad's Wood Road to the north west. This wood was more extensive than Hoad's Wood and is still there today preserved as St.Helen's Park. We normally approached the wood via Langham Road and St. Helen's Wood Road, the latter entirely unadopted and extremely muddy in winter. To the right of this road there is still a dark pond surrounded by trees and sloping fields up to The Ridge. One sunny summer morning, Barry and I stumbled across a whole cluster of large grass snakes, intertwined and absorbing the sun's heat as they lay on the dead bracken fronds at the bottom of the field near the pond. You hear of this phenomenon and we were privileged to witness it, but it aroused that archetypal fear of snakes as we saw a resemblance to a biblical snake pit. A few years later with the permission of the farmer, a Mr Deeprose, I fished the pond using red worms as bait and caught several good sized perch, colourful fish with green and black striped bodies and orange fins, but the dorsal fin has intimidating sharp spines! These fish seemed to appear even more attractive as they were lifted out of the dark water by the crane like action of rod and line, the colourful scales of the fish reflecting the sunlight penetrating through the canopy of alder branches from which insects fell helplessly into the darkness of the pond to be consumed by the fish. To the left of St. Helen's Wood Road, the main woodland sloped away towards a ravine with a stream which like those of the Hoad's Wood area, eventually ends up in Alexandra Park. A part of the stream in St. Helen's Wood flowed through a brick built conduit under a hillock in the wood. We used to dare each other as children to walk, bent over through the narrow conduit. Yet another example of potentially dangerous things children will do, I am guilty to recall the claustrophobic experience.

St. Helen's Wood is an old deciduous woodland containing a typical selection of Wealden trees including oak, holly and beech, and the ground flora includes several species of fern; in autumn there are many species of colourful fungi to be found on the ground and on rotting tree stumps. As far as the fauna are concerned, we never saw any deer, but plenty of grey squirrels. On one occasion we discovered a drey high up in a tree with young just about to leave their home. One or two of the older boys among us, climbed up the tree and and put some of the young squirrels in their jacket pockets. From here they were transported to an empty chicken house in Barry's parents' garden where they were given nuts and water. We used to bring the young squirrels into the dining room where they happily leaped over the furniture and I do not recall anyone being bitten by their sharp teeth. These acquired wild pets remained with us for only a few days before they were released back to the wild in the ravine near Ravine Lodge, next to Barry's family home. There will not be many young grey squirrels who have had that experience with humans, or humans with squirrels!

One other creature localized to specific woods, was the large wood ant, about a centimetre long. I saw a number of these and their nests in a defined part of St. Helen's Wood when I was a child, the area where they were found was where there were pine trees near a footpath, The Drive which led off St. Helen's Park Road to meet St. Helen's Avenue. The wood ants' large nests were often over a metre wide and several centimetres deep and were primarily constructed of pine needles and very small pine twigs. I took some of the ants and their nest material back home in a large jam jar and then watched them reconstruct a nest of tunnels throughout the pine needles before I returned the exiled colony back to the original nest in the woods; what impressed me was the co-operative behavior of these relatively small social insects.

Winter and Christmas was approaching. On a late Saturday

afternoon before Christmas, I would go on my own to St. Helen's Wood equipped with string and my father's secateurs and find some holly laden with red berries which I would cut from the tree and string all the small branches together. The whole would then be flung over my shoulder together with some long vines of ivy to decorate the home for the Christmas period. I suppose today taking these decorations for free would not be approved with the formal organization of a country park and probably rightly so, they should be left for all to appreciate in their natural context and that is a code for not picking many wild flowers.

Beyond St. Helen's Wood were two other places to fascinate the inquiring mind of a growing child, one was in the context of natural history, the other local history. With reference to the natural history experience first, Barry and I were in our early teens and equipped with jam jars and small nets made from mother's discarded nylon stockings and a wire loop fixed to a bamboo cane.. We would walk past St. Helen's Wood and up Hillside Road which was more of a bridal way. Where the road levelled out there was a stile on the left which we climbed over and then walked for about half a mile across meadows towards Hickman's Farm; in the middle field were football pitches of the Grammar School adjacent to the sports field and pavilion to the south, (part of this is now the site of William Parker's School).

When we arrived at the farm, this was the meeting point of three footpaths, the one we had been on, another coming up behind the farm from Old Roar Gill and the third leading away behind the farm to further up the Gill where it became a bridge over the Gill leading to Old Roar Road. In front of the farm buildings at this junction of paths was a small dew pond, providing drinking water for cattle, but more than that the pond contained a text book range of pond life. There was an abundance of oxygenating plants such as Canadian pond weed and starwort and several common or smooth newts, but the biggest attraction was the presence of the

68

now rare great crested or warty newt with its orange and black spotted belly and crested dark back in the male; the male also has a white-blue streak on its tail. Because this newt is confined to a limited number of sites, it is now a protected species. However, over 50 years ago, Barry and I would catch a pair of great crested newts, without difficulty and likewise a pair of smooth newts and together with some water weed and pond snails, we would transport them home in the jam jars. Back home I would put this selection of pond life in a goldfish bowl with some gravel in the bottom and feed the newts on chopped earthworms. But this was only a temporary aquarium, we realized that we should not keep the newts in captivity for too long, just long enough to observe their activity before we took them to small pools in the stream at Scute's Farm. (today, Hickman's Farm and the pond have gone to be replaced by a housing development, only the name of a road Hickman's Way is there to remind us of earlier times).

Hillside Road was not only en route to Hickman's Farm, but it ran north as a track to The Ridge enveloped by a corridor of small trees and bushes. To the east the land immediately fell away to steep sloping pastureland where sheep often grazed. But most importantly was that after a heavy snow fall, these steep fields were excellent for sledging. I can recall the exhilaration of laying on my belly on a home made sledge constructed from spare timber found in the shed at home, and gathering speed by the seconds as the sledge travelled the length of the steep fields. All went well until the sledge hit a mole hill, concealed under the deep snow. The sledge nearly disintegrated and threw me into the snow, legs stinging from the abrasion with the icy 'white stuff' due to me only wearing short flannel trousers until I was 13 (a legacy of Baden Powell's scout movement – all boys must be toughened up!) Surviving such a trauma, the walk back up the hill, time and time again, provided maximum healthy exercise that really did toughen up those young muscles! Incidentally, before 1951 when Hoad's Wood Road was still without tarmac as a rough track, we used to sledge up and down the road in the evenings after school following a snow fall, a good quarter of a mile run with virtually no motor vehicles on the road in those days to obstruct our enjoyment.

The second experience beyond St. Helen's Wood was the one of local historical significance. While I was attending Sunday school at the parish church of St. Helen on The Ridge, I became aware that there was a predecessor of this church, it was the ancient parish church of Ore, now a ruin tucked away in the trees about 400 yards down a track which led off The Ridge by some cottages opposite the Borough cemetery. After Sunday school, I often used to walk down to the ruined church with other boys who lived in Hoad's Wood Road and explore the ruins and churchyard; this was an alternative route to Elphinstone Road. Earlier I mentioned Ore Place where Teilhard de Chardin the theologian, scientist and philosopher trained to be a Jesuit priest at the beginning of the 20th century. This seminary was built in the 1860's next to the earlier Tudor manor house known as Ore Place which in turn was immediately west of the church (fragments of the walls and medieval tiles of the manor house can be seen today via a public access from the new housing development off De Chardin Drive). The church went into disuse in the 1860's with a leaking roof and was replaced by the present St. Helen's Church. Fifty years ago the ruins looked similar to today. All that visibly remains is the west tower, the north wall of the nave and chancel and the east wall and window; much of the masonry is covered with ivy. Within the tower is a spiral staircase and a font. Adjacent to the north wall within the nave is a pulpit built for outdoor services which have occurred from time to time for over a century. The churchyard has many standing head stones, some of notable people buried here who lived in and around Hastings. In a vault under the site of the nave, lies the body of a man of national significance in British history viz. General Murray of Quebec. Another feature once in this church and now sited on a wall in the chancel of St. Helen's Church, is a 15th century brass depicting a man and woman, the woman is notable for the image of the clothing she wears, typical of that for around 1400 AD in England. A recommended read is the short history of the ancient parish church of Ore containing several prints and photographs which have been reproduced, the publication was compiled by the Rev. Canon F.W.B. Bullock in 1949.

Just down the road from the entrance to the track to the ruined church from The Ridge, was a small shop at the top of Elphinstone Road, opposite the Borough Cemetery gates, which conveniently sold flowers. After Sunday school in 1953, a group of us dashed into the shop, excitedly to buy a big bag of liquorice allsorts – sweets after all this time, had just come off war time rationing!

I cannot leave the subject of woodlands without mentioning one wood, which I walked to from Hastings, and this was one of the not previously mentioned excursions with my parents and later my sister Rosalind when I was in my early teens; the venue was Guestling wood about 4 miles from Hoad's Wood Road. We used to ascend to Ore village, then down the other side of the great Ridge along the Rye Road with a right turn at the White Hart Inn down towards Pett village. Before the White Hart Inn, the descending bend from The Ridge is called Bachelor's Bump; here in the garden of a cottage on the left was a pet fox confined to a small wire netted run and kennel; this was the first live fox I had seen, unfortunately not in the wild, but perhaps it had been saved as an orphan after the hunt had killed its mother? On the left before Pett village is Watermill Lane where my grandfather James and his spinster daughter Marjorie, my aunt, moved to a bungalow after grandmother James died in 1953; grandfather James died in 1970 at the good age of 91. I helped to clear up the garden, over grown with grass when the move occurred, unfortunately it was difficult to avoid all the numerous slow worms, those copper coloured, legless lizards hiding in the grass, as I hit the turf with my spade. Just down the road from the bungalow, is Guestling wood where a path tracked down through another typical Wealden wood with a carpet of bluebells, white wood anemones, primroses and bright yellow celandines in the spring. In the depth of the wood we would spread out that war time groundsheet once again for a picnic lunch. From here we would continue to descend down through the wood until we came to a stream which flowed east in the direction of Watermill Lane and at one time would have had enough flow to drive a watermill; eventually the lane goes up hill to meet the Rye Road by the Robin Hood Inn at Icklesham. Our walk continued up a footpath across fields until we came to Guestling Church so typical of rural Sussex with its red tiled pyramid roof on the stout tower – a Sussex cap. Such a tranquil location with only the distinctive call of the cuckoo heard back in the woods we had left behind. From here Church Lane took us back to the Pett Road for the shorter route home, or a longer walk via the Rye Road and detour back south through the hamlet of Three Oaks, across the Four Turnings, past Coghurst Hall and up Ivy house Lane to The Ridge and the final descent to Hoad's Wood Road.

There are two final reflections on going up or down from the family home in Hoad's Wood Road. In the late 1940's there was a triangle of rough grassland at the top of Hoad's Wood Road before the junction with several unadopted roads. On this grass area was a cycle speedway track for a post war craze of racing pedal cycles around a circular track, our local team was called the 'Hoad's Wood Hatchets' who wore images of crossed hatchets on their jackets. There were cycle speedway teams all over the town who raced against each other with tribal fervour. By the early 1950's, this craze had diminished to be replaced by professional motor cycle speedway, and the grass cycle track at the top of Hoad's Wood was replaced by a less aggressive context, the building of St. Barnabas Church, a satellite church for St. Helen's Church. The motor cycle speedway track in Hastings was at the Pilot Field football stadium just north of Hoad's Wood Road and I became a keen supporter of this noisy sport. Two of the Hastings great aces were Wally Green and Ken Middleditch. In each race the four motor cyclists on their JAP bikes kicked up a great spray of ash on the bends as they overtook each other, and the smell of ash and combusted fuel left one with another acute visual experience and olfactory memory of the rich aroma of 'Castrol' lingering in the air.

Another post war event held at the Pilot Field was a military tattoo, I suppose this was a left over from the days of the Empire and having been on the winning side in the recent World War. I, and others, used our tree climbing skills to climb one of the large beech trees on the high bank adjacent to Elphinstone Road and opposite the Pilot Field. Having climbed half way up the tree and settled seated on a large hidden branch, we had a splendid bird's-eye view of the tattoo for free! An associated parade was the gathering of representatives of various military regiments in Alexandra Park on Remembrance Sunday at the War Memorial to lay wreaths of poppies. I remember going to the parade with my parents to watch grandfather Booth file past with the South African war veterans.

The occasion of going down towards the town from Hoad's Wood Road, but not too far, was buying vegetables and fruit from a smallholding 'Yonder Cottage' which was next to the track leading down to Scute's Farm in Elphinstone Road. This smallholding was one of a pair of semi-detached houses, the other being 'Spring Cottage'. 'Yonder Cottage' was run by Fred Weeks and his wife and 'Spring Cottage' by Mrs Campbell and her son Tom. My mother favoured 'Yonder Cottage', although I never knew why. Pigs were kept on both smallholdings, the sties backing on to each other. I used to lean over the low wall of the sty with its rancid, acidic smell of swill prepared from our kitchens' vegetable waste and talk to the white pigs with their comical pig snouts; it was these animals that were my first introduction to this farm animal; I did not know then that one day I would make some fundamental studies on the reproduction of this species. Once or twice during my school holidays when I was at the Grammar School, I did some work on these smallholdings, planting potatoes, weeding in the orchard and hedge cutting to earn some extra money; all good experience for later in life when gardening became a passionate leisure activity for me. Today the smallholdings have gone, but the cottages are part of a housing development.

In addition to fruit and vegetables obtained from 'Yonder Cottage' and father's allotment, the majority of food and other consumables were bought from shops in the suburban area of Mount Pleasant, a hill crowned by Mount Pleasant Congregational Church with a clock on the tall pointed spire – so convenient to see whether I would be late for my respective schools in the area! (Like the fate of so many churches including the Central Methodist Church in Cambridge Road, Mount Pleasant Church was later demolished and replaced by housing). Our grocer's shop was run by the Weeks in Hughenden Road. I was always fascinated when Tom Weeks and his son John disappeared through a trap door in the floor behind the counter to obtain further stocks from the store in the cellar. On the corner of Hughenden Road and Hughenden Place was a hard ware store managed by Mr Brand who wore an old stained apron, as you entered the shop the nose was bombarded by the oily smell of paraffin, polish and creosote. My mother came to this shop for a gallon of paraffin for the free standing heater used in the bathroom, bunches of kindling sticks for the fires and Cardinal red polish for the brick fireplace. Round the corner in Hughenden Place was Gillis's shop (the Gillis family lived next to the Kents in Hoads Wood Road), for further fruit and vegetables and a couple of shops away opposite the Church was Humphrey the butcher who was helped by his sons Bob and Jack. After my parents got married in 1938, their first home was a flat above this butcher's shop before they went to Poole. On the next corner where Hughenden Place meets Mount Pleasant Road, was a chemist's shop, then down hill was the post office managed by Miss White who received either the MBE or OBE for her long years of service to the Post Office. Finally, there was that other shop of convenience, the newsagents Vollers who also sold sweets, tobacco, stationary, small toys, newspapers and magazines; it was from here that I did my paper round.

Three other domestic consumables were delivered to the house from further away. Bread came in a green van from Wicker's in the Old Town. Mr Wicker with his wicker basket of freshly cooked loaves, came round to the back door (which was unlocked if someone was at home), and opened the door calling out in a polite quiet voice "baker"; the order was two large white and a small brown, twice a week. The other deliveries were fuel. Coal, coke and anthracite were delivered by Mr Woodgate and logs came from a number of sources over the years, but always good hard wood from the many trees in the Wealden woods.

By the early 1950's, Hoad's Wood Road was inhabited by a mixed group of essentially home owning people with occupations ranging from the building trade, green grocers, clerical and shop workers, school teachers, writers and artists. The school teachers in addition to those already mentioned, Doug Brightmore and Tom Cookson, were Tom Walsgrove (immediate neighbour down the road from the Cookson's) a maths master at the secondary modern school, John Charrot an English master at the secondary modern school (living just further down the road) and close friend with his wife Margaret, of Tom and Catherine Cookson, and Miss Longhurst teacher at the Mount Pleasant Junior School, who lived at Ravine Lodge; there was also a piano teacher Miss Marjorie Skellorn. Half way up Hoad's Wood Road, just beyond the entrance to Hoad's Wood, lived the Locke sisters, both long retired teachers. These ladies prepared me for a nativity play at St. Helen's Church; I always was the king with the frankincense and a blackened face (produced with vaseline and a burnt cork). An unusual gift from the sisters was an Edwardian, wicker bath chair which I used as a go-cart, up and down Hoad's Wood Road; I suppose I was about 12 at the time. Leading off Hoad's Wood Road was Wilmington Road, the then cul-de-sac off Hoad's Wood Road close to my home with a terrace of late Victorian houses called Weissenburg Terrace, 1870; this was built for brick workers following the Franco-Prussian War, who were employed at kilns north of Hoad's Wood Road, nearby; Hoad's Wood Road was almost a community in its own right.

There were communal Guy Fawkes celebrations in Hoad's Wood Road in the 1940's and '50's with fireworks and the burning of a 'Guy' on a large bonfire built by the school children in the half term break. This also allowed for the roasting of jacket potatoes supplied by the mums and dads, which, when daubed with butter and accompanied by sausages, provided for a warm get together of families on a cold November evening. The site for the bonfire and communal gathering was on waste land at the lower end of Hoad's Wood Road. One year during the days leading up to the 5th November, there was a young Greek Cypriot boy called Nicolas of my age who was staying with Barry's family. We dressed Nicolas up in an old flannel suit with accessories, a trilby hat, old boots and gloves, and placed a pillow case over his head with a Guy's face drawn on it – we had a real Guy! We put Guy Nicolas in an old pram with his limbs dangling over the sides, 'lifeless and limp' and went round the houses calling "Penny for the Guy' please"! Everyone was deceived into thinking this was an excellent stuffed Guy, and our reward was many pennies put towards the purchase of fireworks.

'Shaggy Parasol'

A species of fungi that might be found at the edge of

St. Helen's Wood and pastureland

(photograph of original watercolour by the author)

'Twilight Anticipation'

(photograph of a composition in oils by the author inspired

after fishing in the 'fish pond' off St. Helen's Wood Road in the 1950's)

Ruins of the ancient Parish Church of Ore

as seen from the east end (September 2009)

Remaining wall and archways of the medieval/Tudor manor house

situated SW of the ruined church (September 2009)

78

7. Glens for Inspiration

The Wealden hills surrounding Hastings provide a landscape with numerous ravines created by tumbling streams which have worn away the soft sandstone over millenia and then widened into brooks as the land levels and eventually falls to sea level; here the brooks have become rivers cutting their way through pasture land to the English Channel. It is this landscape which played a significant part of my life as a child offering me fishing venues and natural history.

In Hastings, reference has been made to the streams running south from Hoad's Wood and St. Helen's Wood which merge in the Ore valley and join the stream in Alexandra Park to flow out to sea after passing through a culvert under the main town of Hastings. Similarly, the Old Town of Hastings has its stream, the Bourne, hidden in a culvert under a road before it runs out to sea. East of the Old Town from the East Hill to Cliff End at Pett Level is where the highest hills of the Weald on the coast abruptly meet the sea with falling cliffs alternating with three ravines or glens, and a coastal footpath allows one to readily explore this landscape (since 1991 a Site of Special Scientific Interest – an SSSI).

The first of the glens is Ecclesbourne, readily accessed from the East Hill at Hastings with its stream near its source, dammed to form a reservoir and freshwater fishery. North east of here and the village of Ore, is the highest point on the hills at North Seat reaching 170 metres (seen from Sandhurst, Kent 16 miles away). From here on a clear day one can witness an extensive panoramic view. Twenty miles away to the west, Beachy Head and the South Downs slumber on the horizon while to the north, a view even further across the Weald, to the North Downs beyond Sevenoaks; this line of hills is continued to the east to Folkestone and Dover beyond the vast flat open Romney Marsh and Dungeness, a view over 30 miles away. If the atmospheric conditions are optimum, looking south across the English Channel can be seen France's white cliffs at Cap Gris Nez – I have seen this on a July evening reflecting the sunset over 40 miles away and Europe seemed very close.

Eastwards from Ecclesbourne glen is the most extensive of the glens, this is Fairlight glen. Here is to be found a splended diversity of flora from primitive algae and lichens near the stream including the Dripping Well, to numerous ferns, grasses and flowering plants, indeed a botanist's paradise; the ferns in the glen were commercially exploited in the Victorian era. This 'Garden of Eden' is an ecological niche which set a Grammar School friend of mine, Robert Finch, better known as Bob, on the road to Wadham College, Oxford culminating in a doctorate for botanical research. Bob apart from his career as a scientist working for the government on the genetics of cereals at the Plant Breeding Institute in Cambridge (sadly now closed down), was also an excellent field taxonomist always finding for the first time another moss or lichen in a certain habitat – perhaps normally found in Scotland but now also on the south coast of England, in Fairlight glen. It was a sad event when Bob died of prostate cancer in 2006.

The next glen east along the coast is Warren glen, a much less distinctive dip in the landscape with trees being replaced by bracken and gorse. I can recall this glen in the early 1950's on a school natural history walk being one of the last areas along this coastal strip of cliffs to be cleared of mines placed here for defensive purposes, if the Germans had landed. Furthermore, towards the north of this glen, are old quarries (once providing sand stone for walls in Hastings), and in 1939, a new company the Fairlight Mining Company, leased land between the north of Warren glen and Fairlight Church from a Major Sayer, to dig for sand; the Home Guard used these quarries for rifle practice in the Second World War. Thankfully the coastal path from the East Hill at Hastings to Pett Level has been restored and embraces the Hastings Country Park which is reached by car from a lane leading off the main coastal road at Fairlight church, east of Warren glen with a car park before the coast guard cottages. This area provides another panoramic view to most points of the compass, similar to that seen from North Seat but additionally Rye is clearly visible on a mound crowned by St. Mary's Church and also Romney Marsh (today there is a cluster of wind turbines here producing electrical energy for our urban world from a natural source of power). The view west along the coast from near the coast guard cottages with the Fairlight cliffs in the mid-ground, inspired William Holman Hunt one of the Pre-Raphaelite Brotherhood artists to paint the scene as 'The Coast' or 'Strayed Sheep', a picture now in the Tate Gallery. The immediate area to the coast guard cottages eastwards along the coastal path, is called the fire hills due to the bright yellow colour of the gorse blossom and the fact that the gorse and bracken readily catches alight, often the result of a casually discarded cigarette end.

It is appropriate to refer at this point to two aspects of the conservation of nature with ecological implications and their association with Hastings Country Park, St. Helen's Wood and Ecclesbourne.; both involve ex-Hastings Grammar School boys. The first reference is centred around a boy who attended the Grammar School over a century ago called Archie Bellaney. Archie was absorbed by natural history and spent many hours as a boy in St. Helen's Wood observing and recording wildlife. When he left the Grammar School, Archie emigrated to Canada to become first a hunter, particularly of the beaver and he adopted the life style and dress of a Red Indian claiming to the outside world that he was half Indian and he changed his name to Grey Owl. However, having married a Red Indian girl and producing a daughter, Grey Owl spent the rest of his life endeavouring to save the beaver from being over hunted. Grey Owl wrote several books on his adventures and he became a world pioneer in the promotion of the conservation of wildlife. In the car park next to the visitor centre in the Hastings Country Park at the fire hills, there is a monument with a plague dedicated to Grey Owl.

The second reference of an ecological nature, is the small study my botanist friend Bob Finch and I carried out at Ecclesbourne in 1960 soon after we had left the Grammar School; it was a project suggested by Doug Brightmore our biology master. We looked at the effect of the towns sewage effluent emerging from a pipe on the shore east of the East Hill, on the distribution of flora and fauna between high and low tides. This involved collecting shell fish including molluscs and crustacea, and seaweeds. We then took this array of sea shore life back to Bob's house in Harold Road for identification aided by a hand lens and a microscope mounted on the kitchen table. Bob and I found that the shore life was detrimentally effected by sewage, some species more than others particularly close to the emergence of the effluent; this was an early study on the effect of pollution on wild life and was published in the local natural history magazine ' The Hastings and East Sussex Naturalist' (1966). (Fortunately today the sewage is purified before it enters the sea). Our excursion along the Wealden Coast ends at Pett Level after we have passed through Fairlight Cove, now an extensive area of houses centred around Waites Lane compared with my visit in a thunderstorm as a 3 year old in the War when there were only a few houses, summer chalets and an hotel; I shall return again to Pett Level and the surrounding green pastures later.

There were two people in particular other than my parents who were a great inspiration and encouragement to me while I was at the Grammar School, they were Douglas Brightmore the biology master and Tom Cookson. Earlier Doug had also been an inspiration for another pupil Don Mackean who after Cambridge University and teaching biology, wrote a world's best selling book the 'Introduction to Biology'. Doug was a lean, rugged man - I remember him on his allotment after the War, tanned and wearing shorts. Tom was my fourth year form master and master for 'O' level mathematics; Tom was also the unofficial career's master. He was prone to migraine attacks, probably due to the difficult time at home with his mother-in-law Kate, a woman who had a great influence on her daughter Catherine, the increasingly popular novelist who developed stories around complicated family relationships, many based on her own background. It seemed that during a migraine, Tom could not deal with the mechanics of teaching and went off on a detour about what it means to get good qualifications and obtain an appropriate employment, a very good lesson! Although many biographies have been written about the life of Catherine Cookson which include reference to her husband Tom, I would like to add some further biographical observations about Tom. Tom was an extremely popular master who engaged with the boys in the classroom and outside; his popularity was probably due in part to his 'boyish' countenance, (he also had an extensive model railway laid out in an upper room of his house). Tom was involved with the scouts and football, refereeing the 'scratch sixes' after school on the 'flat' or playground. Tom's enthusiasm for football, I can recall now as he walked by our house in Hoad's Wood Road on a Saturday afternoon dressed in a rain coat, leather gloves and a flat cap - he was on his way to support Hastings United at the Pilot Field. It seems that both Doug Brightmore and Tom Cookson not having children of their own, the school boys were their adopted sons and gave them a 'fatherly' attention. Incidently, Doug Brightmore died in 1979 at the age of 72 and Tom Cookson died 3 weeks after Catherine Cookson in 1998, at the age of 87.

My following poem reflects on the seasonal life cycle of a wild plant, ferns which are found in the woods of Fairlight glen and St. Helen's Wood; philosophical comparisons with the fragility of human life are subtly made:

'Ferns'

Tranquil coolness – they awake from winter slumbers,
Steadily determined crosiers, dull and scaly,
Yet unfolding to a fresh green life on a mouldy, dank, bank;
What bishop's staff can do this?

For fleeting moments, they reflect the sunlight with beams
Of lighter green penetrating the canopy of a higher being, the
hazel.
A sudden breeze, they shudder obstinately
Unmoved by this intrusion in a quiet glade.

The hazel canopy withers, falls, moulds into the dank, bank.
The fern fronds have a bonus,
Defying all but the keenest cold, surviving fronds
Wean the next generation of primordial shapes
Into another season of patterned beauty,
Unchanging, over millennia, contrasting with the whims
Of our fickle existence.

'Midhurst'

Once more we leave the countryside,
The winding roads, and sun,
The quietness of meadows bright
With buttercup and daises white,
Where rivers run.
We look again with wistful eyes
Upon these leafy dales,
The woods, and sunlit hills along
The thicket where we hear the song
Of nightingales.

We visit them in dreams again,
When by the fireside,
We think of flowering chestnut boughs
The little lambs and staring cows,
The valleys wide.
And peace steals gently in our hearts,
Within the clamorous towns,
We see the white-winged clouds at rest
Upon the soft and tender breast
Of Sussex Downs.

© Muriel Hilton

This poem by Muriel Hilton, although depicting a view across the Sussex countryside further west than the Hastings Weald, to the South Downs, this view and atmosphere is comparable to that seen from the high Wealden hills around Hastings.

View from Crowhurst Park to the South Downs and Beachy Head (September 2009).

Also painted by J.M.W. Turner "Pevensey Bay from Crowhurst Park".

View west from Hastings Country Park near the coast guard cottages

to Covehurst and Fairlight glen (September 2009). (The same view was painted

by Holman Hunt and called 'The Coast' or 'Strayed Sheep' in the 19th century)

View east from Hastings Country Park to Rye Bay

and Romney Marsh (September 2009)

Annual cricket match between masters and boys of the
Hastings Grammar School held at the Central Cricket Ground.

L to R: Douglas Brightmore, Harold Bowmer, Tom Cookson

© Sarah Sables

8. Fishing and the Marsh Frog emerges

The year 1953 was a milestone in my life, I had started at the Grammar School and also started that relaxing hobby bringing one close to nature – freshwater fishing. My father had recently handed over to me his war grade black Raleigh bicycle so that I could cycle to school and my grandfather James gave me his 19th century fishing tackle. Grandfather James went into his loft and brought down a hickory 3 piece rod, a brass reel, some feather and cork floats and a Salmon & Glucksteins 'Life Boat' navy cut tobacco tin containing old hooks and weights; the tin had a picture of a life boat being rowed so you can realize the age of the tackle, late 19th century and not used since my grandfather's youth; grandfather said he never went fishing again after he got married in 1902. I still have a float and the tobacco tin, sadly the brass reel with a moulded image of a fisherman casting a line on both sides of the reel suffered metal fatigue and broke; it would have been a collectors piece today. Following the purchase of some monofilament line and a few extra pieces of tackle including a war time respirator bag for my tackle, bought from Malcolm Mitchell's war surplus stores in the Old Town, I lashed my rod to the cross bar of my bicycle and set off for my first fishing trip to the Buckshole reservoir in Alexandra Park; my friend Barry joined me equally tackled up. One summer evening, I remember our main catch with a piece of bread paste was the gudgeon, a colourful little fish with blue markings along a buff coloured body. Other fish were the red finned roach and the deep bronze coloured Crucian carp, but nothing of specimen size. Soon after this Barry and I became junior members of the Clive Vale Angling Club, and I was proud to wear one of those little round lapel badges with the angling club name embedded in green and red enamel. Joining this club widened our horizons for fishing venues which could be reached by bicycle, have a day's fishing and enjoy the countryside. By today's standards, I think the distances we travelled in pursuit of our leisure without mechanized transport, were considerable, but we were young and fit helped by all those years running around the woods, climbing trees etc. Snailham was our favourite destination throughout those teenage years.

Snailham is an area in the valley of the River Brede between Udimore to the north and Icklesham to the south. Our 6 mile cycle journey took us via Ore and down hill to Guestling on the Rye Road to Icklesham, or sometimes we passed St. Helen's Church and turned right down Chown's Hill to Ivy House Lane and passed Coghurst Hall to the hamlet of Three Oaks before reaching the Rye Road near Icklesham. At this village we turned left down Broad Street then up a track through a farm before the track took us down through a steep banked area with white violets in Spring, into the Brede valley at Snailham Halt; this was a stop for steam trains on the route from Hastings to Ashford. (Today, neither the steam train nor the Halt are there, just a diesel train with fewer stops along the line).

A grass track took us across pasture land in the valley over the 'First' dyke to a copse of hawthorn trees by Langford Bridge which was a precarious old wooden structure over the River Brede. Here we would leave our bicycles for several hours with no locks, but they were rarely out of site as we chose our fishing spots. These would be either the main river if the lock gates further down the valley were closed to hold the water back, or to the 'First' dyke; in the autumn and winter, the 'Third' dyke nearest to Udimore was popular because eatable jack pike weighing just a few pounds were abundant here. The 'First' dyke probably provided us with the most sport using bread paste or red worms dug from a compost heap back home. Species we caught were roach, silver bream, rudd, perch and pike. The main river provided mostly roach and common bream while the 'Third' dyke in addition to the pike had some good tench; this fish is known as the 'doctor' fish due to the supposed property of the mucous covering its body in healing other fish.

After a couple of years, I bought my first coarse fishing rod with my pocket money for under £1 from Redfearns the tackle shop in Hastings (it was still there recently, in Castle Street). The rod was made from a copper aerial, probably made for radio communication in military tanks in the War, inserted into a wooden handle producing a one piece unit. My first outing with this rod was further up the Brede Valley near the bridge on the main road from Hastings to Northiam via Brede village. Doug Brightmore my Grammar School master was now living with his wife Dorothy at Little Knights Farm, a smallholding just up the hill from the Brede Bridge as you travelled from Hastings. A few yards down from the bridge early one weekend morning, I Christened my new rod by catching a good bream over 3 lbs but it seemed much bigger than this on my small rod as it bent into a semi-circle! I had just caught the largest bream for the season as a junior member of the Clive Vale Angling Club.

Back to Snailham on a cold early January Saturday in 1955. Barry and I had decided to go pike fishing in the 'First' dyke before we realized that this was not the best water for this fish at Snailham. The method we were going to use was dead baiting, but first we had to catch a reliable supply of small fish for the bait. The previous summer we had discovered a small pond known as Cook's pond at the top of a field south of Icklesham off Pannel Lane, the road between Icklesham and Pett village, about 5 miles from Hastings which cuts across the valley of the Pannel sewer; this water course is the outcome of the watershed of Guestling woods and eventually drains into the Military Canal at Pett Level. Cook's pond was full of stunted rudd and tench, apparently fertile as they had roes, seen when the fish were taken home and cooked for the cat; the small size of the fish was likely to be due to over population stretching the natural food resources of the pond, another indicator of fertility. A lovely spot to fish seated among the marginal reeds in the Sussex countryside with no sound of traffic or people, only the wildlife. You could catch over 50 rudd a day here, ideal for catching a fraction of this in an hour or so to use for pike fishing at Snailham.

Barry and I having caught our quota of rudd at Cook's pond for pike fishing, went on our way for another couple of miles to Snailham, passing the windmill at the top of the hill where today Sir Paul McCartney has his recording studio at the converted mill house. Then on through Icklesham to Snailham. Barry and I would then 'tackle up' using a large cork float, painted green and orange (which I still have after over 50 years, but not used), and the two trebled hooked 'Jardine' snap tackle with a small rudd impaled on the two smaller hooks of each treble. On one occasion we sat by the 'First' dyke' without a 'run' under leaden skies, and a temperature near to freezing with a biting wind. My mother told me afterwards, that while walking to the shops she met Barry's father who said, *"those boys must be out of their minds undertaking such a trip in this weather"*, now I have to agree! We had learned our lesson, we did not go pike fishing on such cold days again. There were many more comfortable days of pike fishing to be had and we liked to catch a fish of 2-5 lb, these were best for eating after soaking cutlets in salt water overnight and then baking them in butter and parsley – delicious apart from the numerous small 'Y' shaped bones! An aspect that insured a good flavour was the dykes being surrounded by only pasture, no run off, of agricultural chemicals, and no boat traffic.

By the summer of 1956, I had bought another rod from Redfearns, this time for £5, it was a 3 piece single cane rod, (I still have this and occasionally use it). Barry, now left school and working for his father in the plastering trade, was earning money, this meant he could afford to buy a good quality split cane rod. Did he catch more fish than me? I think we were about the same, but Barry's rod handled better than mine and over the years with many rods since those days, his catches of numerous double figure carp have certainly made him the serious coarse fisherman that I did not sustain into adulthood. It is worth mentioning here that another piece of important tackle, the fixed spool reel was just emerging on the angling scene and Barry and I bought our first junior forms enabling us to cast further with ease.

Sometimes when fishing went rather quiet, Barry and I did what we used to do when we were younger, we went exploring. Two of these excursions come to mind. One was walking across the pastures and over the 'Third' dyke towards Udimore and stumbling across Great Park Wood on the northern slopes of the Brede valley. Once in the wood we were suddenly aware of loud croaking in the tops of the tall trees, as we looked up there to our amazement were the enormous nests of the grey heron. Like anyone else whose has seen the heron standing like a statue by a pond or river waiting for its prey of fish or frog, to find a heronry is a contrasting experience to the quietness of the countryside around – a hive of great activity in a big way, large birds swooping into the tops of the tall trees to build their large nests of twigs or feed the young once the nests are completed; I wish I had had a camera to record the scene.

The second diversion away from fishing and going for a walk, led to the gruesome finding of a sheep's skull, I had to add this to my collection of animal skulls at home as a budding zoologist. I somehow took the skull home as it was essentially now just bone, and removed the remaining fat with washing powder in my mother's washing boiler, I think on this occasion, mother was very lenient and understanding of my requirements!

More aesthetic was the almost continuous echoing calls of living sheep across the Snailham levels particularly when they had lambs; today this sound brings back nostalgic memories of those fishing days, (or more recently my association with farm animals in my research career). Another haunting sound at Snailham, notably as dusk began to fall in the autumn, was the plaintive call of the lapwings as flocks of these birds glided from one field to another, alas a more rare sight today. Then there were the cattle. There seemed to be an almost resident herd of Sussex cattle in a field between Langford bridge and the lock gate down the valley. These cattle are a beautiful dark red-brown and what we saw was a proud bull with a harem of about a dozen cows. We were always very wary of the bull, and kept to the other side of the field if we decided to move on to another fishing spot which necessitated passing through this field, however the bull fortunately seemed to totally ignore us.

Having arrived at the lock or rather better called a sluice gate on the River Brede, there are two further memories which then were a new experience to Barry and I. On a wall of the sluice gate on the down flow side of the gate, was an extensive growth of algae and slithering up through this matted greenery were hundreds of young eels called elvers, each just a few inches long looking like thick silver wire. These snake-like fish were migrating into the hinterland to seek a variety of suitable water habitats (sadly today, eels have become more scarce). The remaining experience down stream of the sluice, was early one Sunday morning when Barry and I had made an extra effort to get up early and cycle to Snailham, we saw a couple of sea trout moving along the river under the opposite bank, we never saw this species again on our fishing trips; (it was many years later when taking holidays with my own family in North Wales that I saw sea trout again).

Finally before leaving Snailham, I must recall a couple of other experiences involving cattle. Apart from the Sussex herd, other cattle were bullocks being fattened for meat. One day Barry and I were sitting, fishing on top of the bank of the main river when an inquisitive bullock crept up behind me and grabbed my canvas rod case laying on the grass, in its mouth. I immediately tried to retrieve the case. but to no avail, the mischievous bovine galloped off across the field slowly swallowing the whole case out of site into its stomach! Needless to say, at the end of the day I had to get my 3 piece rod home without it being contained in its case, somehow tied to the cross bar of the bike. The following week when we returned to the same part of the river, there in the middle of the field was my regurgitated rod case, obviously resistant to the corrosive stomach juices of the bullock, but now no longer any use to me either!

The other incident with bullocks, was as Barry and I were returning home on our bikes across the marshes, and just before we reached the level crossing gates at Snailham halt, a herd of obstreperous bullocks chased us and we were forced to abandon the bikes and leap up on the gates to safety. Fortunately, the animals soon got bored like young youths and wandered off from whence they came so that we could retrieve our wheeled steeds and go home. But the encounter with bullocks does not quite end here. When Barry and I went to collect our bikes from the hawthorn copse by the river at the end of another day, a bullock had knocked over one of the bikes and trodden on one of the wheels, giving it a slight buckle but not bad enough to prevent the bike from being ridden home. We leave Snailham with its autumn sunset and the silhouette of a girl riding a horse along the track across the fields, the night mist was forming from the ground upwards and enveloping the horse and rider providing a ghostly image fading into the mist.

Barry and I once fished in the Military Canal at Pett Level near the Colonel Body Memorial Lakes which are a bird sanctuary. A more expansive landscape than Snailham, but I do not recall that the fishing was exceptional. However, there is often a compensation for lack of fish, with other wildlife to be appreciated. Here in late June there was an abundance of our native white water lily in bloom, it was the first time I became aware that these beautiful floating flowers, with petals like swan's wings when closed, have a distinctly rose-like scent. Another discovery for us here in the dykes was the presence of the introduced, floating water fern *Azolla filiculoides* originating from North America; this essentially attractive plant turning from green to red, is an ecological problem in some locations because it forms extensive mats reducing the light beneath it and affecting the progress of submerged life forms.

Moving further east, we left the Wealden hills behind us as Barry and I made fishing trips to Carter's gravel pits beyond Camber Castle, one of Henry VIII's coastal forts. To get to these waters, we had to cycle to the ancient town of Rye and take the road to Rye Harbour, the pits were on the right about half way along the road, about 11 miles from Hastings. Apart from fishing for the usual range of smaller coarse fish in the gravel pits, in the dykes nearby was another small fish, the three-spined stickleback. Barry and I made a special trip to catch some of these attractive and darting fish, in children's shrimp nets, and take them home in our usual transporting aquarium tanks, jam jars with lids punctured with small holes for air to enter. Like the observations on the great crested newts, we noted the breeding behaviour of the sticklebacks in my gold fish bowl. The females are pale coloured, whereas the males in the breeding season are highly colourful with blue-grey backs and scarlet bellies and are very aggressive, courting the females and attacking other males for dominance. The males also construct nests for several females to lay their eggs in, before they are fertilized by the milt from the males. We observed the elements of nest building as the male made an impression in the sand at the bottom of the gold fish bowl by using the wafting action of its pectoral fins and also shifting the sand with the current created by its gill motions; small pieces of water weed would then be carried in the mouth and laid in the cauldron in the sand.

But, the most intriguing event experienced in the dykes near Carter's gravel pits, was Barry's and my first contact with the Hungarian marsh frog *Rana ridibunda,* our largest amphibian. This frog was introduced into the Romney marsh area from eastern Europe in 1935 and has spread outwards from here into the lower regions of the valleys of rivers such as the Rother and Brede; when we witnessed the species in the mid-1950's, it had migrated to the south side of the Rother near the coast. Our introduction to the marsh frog was on hearing a chirping croak not unlike the call of the moorhen, coming from one of the dykes. As we cautiously approached the dyke on our hands and knees, in the direction of this unusual sound, there emerging from a bed of water weed was the head of this large frog with its air sacs rhythmically bulging like the cheeks of a trumpet player; this was a male full of testosterone letting the females know of his whereabouts, and of course competing males. Then, somehow I was able to imitate the croak of this frog and a most extraordinary happening occurred, the frog stopped croaking and swam across the dyke towards us and started to crawl up the bank of the dyke continuing its hypnotized progression in our direction! As soon as I stood up in amazement with this behaviour, the frog about turned and plunged back into the dyke, it knew it had met its match! Such are the fascinating and unplanned exposures to nature, on this occasion I had achieved an event known as mimicry, in this case me as another larger 'male frog'!

Other fishing excursions to river valleys draining the eastern slopes of the Weald were to the River Brede downstream from Snailham near Winchelsea. Here I caught and ate my first coarse fish other than pike, it was some roach. Although not considered to be particularly palatable, tasting muddy like the tendancy of many coarse fish as opposed to game fish such as trout and salmon, these roach were surprisingly sweet in flavour, more like a sea fish but it was the vast number of small bones, again as in the pike, that spoiled the occasion. Further afield, Barry and I cycled to the River Rother at Bodiam, not seriously to fish with rod and line but to catch minnows in a net and transport them back home in our jam jars to closely observing their behaviour in that perennial gold fish bowl. After a day's coarse fishing on a Sunday in the mid-'50's, I would eat my reheated Sunday roast on my lap in front of a welcoming open fire and listen to Sir Bernard Lovell on the wireless, giving the Reith lecture on astronomy. Sir Bernard's rich lilting voice expounding on the Universe with recent information arising from the new radio telescopes, was a great inspiration for a young school boy adding more meaning to the physics lesson the next day.

Barry and I now started to turn our attention to another species to fish, it was the brown trout, not in the manner of using an artificial fly resembling a naturally occurring insect, the 'proper' way to fish for game fish, but by the country boy's method – using a red worm. In pursuit of this new quarry for us, we set forth on our longest cycle ride to fish, a good 18 miles in each direction, by going north, up and down the hills of the Weald to the Rother again, but further upstream from Bodiam and beyond Robersbridge; this was Etchingham where there were supposed to be a few trout and the flow of water became more positive, an important characteristic of trout waters because the greater the turbulence the more oxygen is absorbed, vital for active fish like trout. We were using our coarse fishing tackle but with a small, light float and of course a small red worm. We walked up and down the river all day without a fish for the bag and another exhausting cycle ride home. To add to my fruitless day, I had the worst 'bird's nest' in my fishing experience., you do not catch a bird's nest, you acquire it, an insoluble tangle of fishing line where you have to cut and sacrifice differing amounts of fishing line; we never went to this water again.

Of all the fishing I did, I found the pursuit of the brown trout the most appealing, and I still do, with something to put in the frying pan and enjoy as a meal at the end of the day. To me this is what hunting, shooting and fishing should be about, not just the sport for its own sake, but something to eat as the end point to satisfy a basic survival instinct. After the abortive excursion for trout at Etchingham, we were informed about another water nearer to home (about 6 miles) where trout existed, this was the River Line, we knew this river further downstream as the River Brede. This upper reach of the River Brede is a small brook fed by two feeder streams, the main one originating near Mountfield, the other near

Battle to form the River Line which flows from Whatlington to Sedlescombe. Our introduction to this upper stretch of the Brede valley was through a boy at the Grammar School whose father somehow knew that there were trout here accessed by a public right of way along the river. Barry and I cycled out to Whatlington one Saturday afternoon and leaned over the red brick road bridge over the River Line – straight away we saw a small brown trout suspended a few inches below the surface of the water, facing up stream as it was spot-lighted by the sunlight beaming through a gap in the over hanging alder tree. That was it! Barry and I were soon to make a return visit to this watery paradise to fish for brown trout over a number of seasons.

By now, my copper aerial rod once used for coarse fishing, was now given a cork handle from a friend to become a short trout rod for the worming method, the short rod was ideal for placing it between the alder branches overlapping the river which was no more than two metres wide in most places. We would cycle north from Hastings along the A21 on the London Road for about 5 miles until we got to the road bridge where the River Brede becomes the River Line, upstream from the Waterfall Tea Gardens mentioned earlier. We left our bikes under a hedge at the edge of a field next to the A21 and started fishing along the River Line upstream towards Whatlington, trying likely spots holding fish such as gaps in the trees with small eddies. The edge of Petley Wood on our left came down to the river and the coppiced wood of hazel was slowly combusted to charcoal on smoking heaps; this aromatic smoke combined with the pungent yet wholesome smell of wild garlic, added to the later nostalgic memory of this experience. Apart from the copper rod, the remainder of the tackle included an early fixed spool reel, monofilament line, a very small green and white cork float (still in my possession) and a size 12 hook; the bait of red worms was retrieved from a compost or leaf mould heap back home. We would cast the worm upstream in an eddy or cutting under a bank where we expected the trout to lie, a take of the worm resulted in a sudden movement of the float upstream into the depths of the pool - then you struck with the rod. The trout were never very large, 6 to 8 inches on average with those distinctive colours of a typical wild brown trout, a gold and silver body covered with red and brown spots, a green, brown dorsal area camouflaging the fish in the water. The experiences of fishing for trout in the River Line are condensed in the following poem:

'Sedlescombe to Whatlington'

Between Whatlington and Sedlescombe there flows an
Alder-lined stream,
Winding through a gentle Sussex valley, to me now just a
Dream.
Once reality, a Saturday or a Sunday, sometimes an
Evening too,
I cycled there 6 miles from Hastings, to catch a trout or two.
Such was the vigour and expectancy of youth
With retreats by the stream to soothe,
Like the sequence of spring flowers,
'O' levels, 'A' levels, paper round, jazz clubs, coffee
Bars and girls.

Bike parked under a hedge, I 'tackled up' a simple rod and line,
Partly a copper aerial with a cork butt, monofilament,
Small float and a brandling worm.
Stealthily I moved upstream along the grassy bank,
Wondering where a trout might be to take

The worm as it sank.
The stream was too intimate to wade in, overgrown
With alder, figwort and briar,
So from the bank I searched for pools where an
Anticipated trout might lie.
Suddenly – here was the spot, perfect in every way,
The smell of ransomes, a blackbird singing, charcoal
Burning amongst bluebells,
It was the month of May.

On a bend in the stream, the current slowed and sticks
And debris were halted,
By a fallen branch jammed perpendicular to the bank,
With the alder roots it courted.
I cast upstream to the foyer of the pool, the worm sank
Fast or slow,
Depending on the current and the magnitude of flow.
Perhaps a few minutes or no time at all,
The white-green float darted upstream to the beginning
Of the pool.
The rod reflexed in action, bent back to the over hanging
Trees,
My heart was pounding with excitement, landing net ready,
As I went down on my knees.

An enormous tug, a flash of gold in the darkness under
The bank,

Then the darkness, darkened, nothing moved or could be
Moved, the fleeting moments of expectancy sank, dank.
Not for the fish, but me as it had thrown the hook
Cunningly it seemed entwining it to the alder roots of the brook.
Mirroring life, no gain this time, one step forward, two
Steps back,
Loss of trout and a bit of tack.
But the day was young and so was I, disappointment soon
Transposed to joy with many pools yet to try,
Each with a trout, unending nature, bombarding nose, ear
And eye.

All emotions were in this valley, too many to define or
Understand,
The contrasts of anticipation and reflection always took
Command.
I responded, in my tackle bag (for a gas mask a decade ago),
Was a cherry wood pipe, some 'Cut Golden Bar' and matches
To make it glow.
With pipe in mouth, my charcoal burner adding aroma
To those sensuous days of spring,
I put on a new hook and baited up, with another brandling
From the moss in the tin.
Yet another hurdle to overcome between stream and a
Marshy glade,
Was a fence like a groin, linking sea and a South
Coast promenade.

Over the fence first went the tackle,
Then I leaped – skimming green algae, rusty nails,
What a spectacle!
To the right, the marshy glade reflected magic – golden
King cups in clumps standing proud,
Above beds of spongy sphagnum moss and peppermint,
Drinking the iron – stained liquor of the Weald.
To the left, my dream stream straightened with a necklace
Of pools and steep banks,
It was here that the worm was taken and fish caught, more
Often than drawing a blank.
If here for a day, I might be half way between Sedlescombe
And Whatlington at noon,
Another hour of casting upstream then my turn for a bite,
Scrambled egg sandwiches and a homemade macaroon.

These regular delights packed at dawn in a regular 'Oxo'
Tin,
Washed down with diluted orange juice in a blue-capped
Bottle supplied free for my younger kin.
With one of nature's appetites satisfied by this humble
Feast,
I continued upstream to Whatlington along meadows
Embracing curves of the brook, not least,
Because here in this small Sussex valley,
The warming sun came forth to rally,
From behind a leaden cloud,

All scents and sounds of nature – buds bursting and
Pheasants cackling aloud.

One last pool before the road bridge, Whatlington at last!
I poked my rod tip through the alder twigs to make a
Final cast.
The sun was setting down for the night behind woods
North of Battle,
Sounds dominant now, only the roosting alarm of
Blackbirds and the distant lowing of cattle.
For a second time that day, my rod and line went taught
As once again a good sized trout took all, but this time
It was caught!
The textbook time for catching a monster – evening, all
Images blurred by fading light,
Into the net the monster slipped from its starwort home,
Fright, fight then night.

For me, this time, not the frantic casts at dusk to
Catch the fish not caught all day,
I had a 'pounder' in the bag and six others, smaller, gold
And silver, with red spots – I was on my way.
Back to the War grade Raleigh, hoping it would still be there
But why not, no locks and chains in those days, people
Had more care.
Rod strung to cross bar, saddlebag full, with an evening meal,
The hunter returned to Hastings, ascending Ebden's hill,

As darkness descended, front and rear lights on,
More study, jazz, coffee bars, girls and neon.

One of the largest brown trout caught by me over 50 years ago in East Sussex, was on a trip to Sailor's stream near Doleham Halt, the railway stop before Snailham Halt travelling from Hastings. Sailor's stream is very small originating from the lakes at Coghurst Hall and streams from The Ridge which cross Stonestile Lane running north into a small valley at the hamlet of Three Oaks. The stream then passes by the old house Great Maxfields before entering a wider valley at Doleham and finally joining the River Brede west of Snailham. At Doleham where Sailor's stream is known as the Doleham Ditch, it enters open pasture land, here there are a few pools and it was in one of these that I caught a 12 inch, 1 lb brown trout – a good size for such a small water. Unlike the dash of a hooked trout, is the slow nibble of that 'toad like' small brown fish with a large head and small body, the miller's thumb or bullhead. This little fish laying on the bottom occasionally took the worm in the River Line, as did another small plain fish, the stone loach.

There is one other river valley to comment on, and that is the River Tillingham running north of Udimore which like the River Brede, also joins the Rother near Rye; I visited this with some other lads one Saturday afternoon travelling there by motorized transport. This was not a fishing trip, just an afternoon's outing to the countryside. The lane we finally took to the Tillingham valley from Udimore, went down through Great Sowden Wood. The lane then continues up hill from the valley in the direction of Beckley Woods and Beckley Furnace so named because once iron ore was processed here into ingots by the heat of charcoal. The River Tillingham here is more of a stream, not a stretch for fishing. However, we witnessed an unusual occurrence. Clinging to the stones by their mouths, on the bottom of the very shallow water were a number of brook lampreys, those primitive eel-like fish without the bones of the more advanced fish we fished for. Lamprey are apparently edible, but perhaps in limited numbers because Henry I is reported to have died from eating too many of the creatures. At least I had survived the eating of some coarse fish.

Although as a child time seemed endless, looking back at the years spent fishing in the ponds, rivers and streams of the Weald near Hastings, it soon passed. Barry being older than me went away on National Service while I was becoming more involved with my studies at the Grammar School and the 'O' level and 'A' level examinations to pass. However, I had the opportunity to combine 'business ' with pleasure. When I was studying for my 'A' level botany, I used to go trout fishing on the River Line and at the same time collect flowers for taking back to the biology class room and drawing floral diagrams to show the basic structure of flowers within each classification of families.

I cannot leave the subject of fishing without reference to a marvellous paper back book 'Mr Crabtree Goes Fishing' which is a 20th century follow on from Izaak Walton's 17th century book 'The Complete Angler'. 'Mr Crabtree Goes Fishing' was written by that angler, expressive writer and artist, Bernard Venables who died at the age of 94 in 2001. The book was first published in 1949 and arose from the strip cartoons which Bernard Venables wrote and illustrated on fishing in the Daily Mirror during the 1940's. In brief, the book involves a pipe smoking father introducing his son Peter to fishing for different species of freshwater fish through the seasons of the year. The true to life descriptive cartoon drawings and wonderful colour illustrations of fish, backed up by concise details in a short text on how to fish and the tackle required, was a young fisherman's 'Bible'. I bought my copy in 1956 and thousands of copies were sold making it a fishing best seller. In celebration of the 50th anniversary since the first publication of the book, a facsimile copy was produced in the year 2000.

Looking towards Udimore, Barry anticipating a bite
in the 'First Dyke', Snailham (August 1956).

Looking east to the old wooden Langford Bridge
over the River Brede, Snailham (July 1956).

View of the Brede Valley looking west towards Snailham

from Float Lane, Udimore (July 1994).

Looking west across Cook's Pond, Icklesham (September 1956)

Looking east from Whatlington towards Sedlescombe

with the River Line within the mid-view of trees (August 1991).

The Hungarian marsh frog emerges from the dyke up the bank towards the "croaks" made by the author (right), while Barry looks on in amazement (left).

9. "Down the town"

"Down the town" was a standard phrase used by those living in suburbia and the answer to the following type of question in every day conversation. *"Where are you going?" "Where is he or she?" "Where did you see so and so?"* - *"Down the town"*. It seemed that we were going somewhere, where the needs of every day life and entertainment could be found, shops, schools, churches, the seaside, museums, libraries, cinemas, etc. not least people.

Earlier I mentioned the walking trips with my parents to certain areas in and around the town i.e. Alexandra Park and the Old Town, and catching buses or trains to go beyond the environs of Hastings. There were two notable events in the calendar which involved me going in to town with my parents, one was the annual town carnival held in July. With my father now the manager of Hepworths the retail tailor in the lower part of Queen's Road between the Town Hall and the Memorial clock, we had a 'bird's eye' view of the carnival procession as it came down Queen's Road from its starting point in Alexandra Park. We sat in the bay window on the first floor of the shop which overhung the road above the milling crowd below, and received a targeted wave and smile from the newly crowned and glamorous carnival queen enthroned on a float where the back of a lorry had been turned into a stage adorned with flowers, ladies in waiting and court jesters. We were fortunate to have this unique view, because the carnival procession was held on a Wednesday afternoon, early closing for the shops including Hepworths. This meant we had the shop to ourselves with father off work for the afternoon, and me also when I was at the Grammar School which also had Wednesday afternoon off (associated with in the past, many local business men's boys going to the Grammar School).

After the long procession had past with its numerous floats representing local businesses and other organisations, the family made its way on foot up Cambridge Road to the Oval, the large area of recreation ground where the carnival fair had just started up. This was my first experience of a large fair ground where at the entrances there were candy floss and toffee apples to tempt the young sweet tooth, and provide energy for the various rides on fast round-a-bouts, dodgem cars and large colourful swing boats with their woolly pull ropes to get you high in the air; passive entertainment was provided by the wall of death motor cycles, a ghost train and various side shows. This entertainment was more impressive than just the dodgem cars and penny-in-the-slot machines I visited without parents, but with friends at the amusement arcades on the Pier or in George Street.

The other annual event in town was the Guy Fawkes celebrations on a Saturday nearest to the 5th November. Again we watched the procession from the bay window above father's shop as it occurred in the evening after the shop was closed, and being November it was dark. I recall how sinister the tall, stuffed guys looked, each produced by one of the bonfire boys' groups around the town (grandfather James in his younger days used to belong to the Ore bonfire boys' club). The awesome appearance of the guys was due to their height, chained to the back of a lorry, and their tall black hats just missing the trolley bus wires. The heads were made of papier mache with black bearded faces and staring eyes giving the impression they were going to their execution; these heads were removed and kept from year to year while the rest of the body was burnt on an enormous bonfire on the beach. The whole spectacle was accompanied by the letting off, of fireworks, and torch bearers, but nothing like the magnitude to be experienced at the small town of Battle 6 miles away. But there was a Guy Fawkes celebration nearer to home which was held at Kemp's Field off Rock Lane in Ore village. In my final 'O' level year at the Grammar School and studying chemistry, I visited the house of a school friend Bob Davis who lived in a house opposite Ivy House Lane on The Ridge, to do revision together. A few days before 5th November, a group of us produced some home made fireworks in

Bob Davis's parents' shed using weed killer potassium chlorate, sulphur and fine charcoal (essentially an explosive mixture!)- these components purchased from a gardening shop and the chemist. On the night of the Kemp's Field celebrations, we took our home made fireworks to the event and ignited them a little away from the crowds, fortunately there were no nasty explosions, just large yellow-green flares producing rather choking suphurous fumes which were diluted by smoke from proper fireworks and the bonfire – so no real harm done!

I have mentioned that as young as 8 years old, I went into town with other young children on Saturday mornings to the ABC minors at the 'Ritz' cinema, then being a little older, I spent a short time in amusement arcades, a relatively innocent novelty, but soon abandoned. Apart from these events, one special occasion I can recall, was the visit to the Central Cricket Ground of the then Princess Elizabeth in 1951, two years before she was crowned Queen. All the schools including me turned out to see the young Princess walking elegantly around this large area of green grass right in the town centre many years before it became the Priory Meadows shopping centre (this cricket ground was one of the top grounds in England used for senior county matches including of course, Sussex). The other Royal event was four years earlier following the wedding of Princess Elizabeth to Prince Philip. The schools went to that other ABC cinema, the 'Regal' in London Road, St. Leonards to see a technicolour film of the wedding, but for me, an important feature of the outing was to see and hear the illuminated cinema organ as it emerged from the floor with changing green and red lights at the front of the 'art deco' cinema, (both ABC cinemas were demolished many years ago).

Also in 1951, this was the year of the Festival of Britain which was a reflection of Britain's increasing economic confidence and a boost to the morale of the nation following the bleak years of the War, less than a decade earlier. I was in the fourth and final year of Mount Pleasant Junior School. During this year, apart from sitting the 11 plus examination, in art lessons we were preparing for the Festival of Britain insofar as each pupil made a folder for keeping all the leaflets and newspaper cuttings about the pending Festival which was to be focused on a bomb site area, the South Bank of the River Thames in London.

Our school I suppose was one of many within a day trip from London, which made its outing venue for 1951, the Festival of Britain. Our 6 school coaches arrived at this awesome sight with its massive Dome of Discovery containing exhibitions on the latest scientific discoveries, and the Skylon that sky scraper high, cigar like structure supported on metal stilts standing as the land mark of the site; I remember standing right underneath the Skylon so that all you could see looking up was a 'large ball', really the maximum diameter of the elongated cone structure, tens of feet directly above me. On the return journey home, we stopped at Hildenborough near Sevenoaks so that all the children could stretch their legs and rush to a stall to buy a brown paper bag full of ripe, red Kent cherries – at the peak of their season. On the bus once again to complete the final part of the journey back to Hastings, the children indulged in the cherries interrupted by bouts of the usual sing-songs; arriving at Manor Road outside Mount Pleasant Junior school, we fell into the arms of our anxiously waiting parents, utterly exhausted.

Two years after the Festival of Britain was the coronation of Queen Elizabeth II on 2 June 1953. That day in Hastings,started with grey skies and rain, and the schools had a holiday. My friend Barry and I had decided to have tortoises as pets, and so we set off on our bikes in the pouring rain to Bexhill (I assume somehow we knew there were tortoises in a pet shop here and not in the pet shop in the High Street of the Old Town in Hastings). I remember the 6 mile journey to Bexhill seemed endless as the rain lashed down on us pushing our pedals along the long straight Bexhill Road. Eventually we got to the old town area of Bexhill to the north of the main town, and Barry and I each bought a pair of tortoises and returned home thoroughly soaked, with these reptilian pets in our saddle bags; kept in small runs in our gardens, these pets gave us further opportunities to study animal behaviour particularly how tortoises attempt to produce another generation – with some cumbersome difficulty! By early afternoon the sun emerged, and all the school children congregated on the large lawn in the lower part of Alexandra Park near the Park cross roads; here there was dancing and various festive events to mark the great day for the Queen and the nation. A Coronation Souvenir Book was given by the Borough Council to all school children.

One particular shopping trip with my mother, often in school holidays, was to a couple of brothers who had a fish barrow covered with freshly caught fish from the fish market in the Old Town; the barrow was just off Queen's Road round the corner by the Cricket Ground, in South Terrace. A favourite buy was dabs, a flat fish, so fresh that their tails curled up in the frying pan, cooked either in batter or a dusting of flour; (today living a long way from the coast, such a fresh luxury is only a dream). Another cheap buy, mild and sweet, was the whiting.

In the fourth year at the Grammar School when I was sixteen in 1956, I started going out with the lads and lasses on the occasional evening and at the weekends into town.; prior to this in my early teens, once a week I only went to the Sunday school mid-week club where we played table tennis, billiards and undertook some carpentry making egg stands and similar simple domestic items. The occasional evening out as a 16 year old, was in summer, on a Wednesday evening. We went to an event which was suitable for most ages, dancing and fireworks in Alexandra Park. The dancing was held on the large lawn near the Park Gates and one of the bands I recall, was Jimmy Shand's with his accordion. As soon as the light began to fade into darkness, the dancing ceased and the crowd went and sat on the high bank above the boating lake to watch a firework display. The themes of the display over the boating lake, were various, one for example was two boxers, the outline of their bodies illuminated by fireworks as their puppet like bodies oscillated with their attempts to score points. It was on one of these evenings that I tried my first cigarette and saw a girl I rather fancied, but it was to be another couple of years before a girl seriously came my way, I was too involved with my 'A' level studies. If not in person at the dancing and firework display in the Park, I could hear the music and fireworks a mile away from the dining room at Hoad's Wood Road, particularly when the casement windows were open on a warm July evening and the incessant chirping of the dark bush crickets in the rose bushes competed with the distant sound of the urban entertainment.

The 1950's was the decade when popular music changed from the crooning of individual ballard singers i.e. Bing Crosby, Frank Sinatra and Frankie Lane, Johnny Ray or group singers such as the Beverly Sisters (accompanied by either an orchestra, a big band or combo), to a lead singer often playing a guitar accompanied by other guitars, a double bass, drums and a saxophone or two. The unforgettable example of this was Bill Haley and his Comets, that revolutionary new sound from America called Rock n' Roll; it hit the charts with 'Rock Around the Clock' and every teenager flocked to their local record shop to buy a 45 rpm vinyl disc. In Hastings a main record shop was the Disc Jockey in the High Street, in the Old Town, soon to be followed by other Disc Jockeys in Queen's Road and King's Road, all pioneered by John Hodgson a later promoter of the Dolphin Jazz Band and several times Mayor of Hastings. Records were soon to be followed by films. Who could resist a visit to the cinema to see the gyrations of Bill Haley with his 'kiss curl' and jiving couples on the dance floor? Unfortunately, the audience at some cinemas could not contain their excitement and the furniture suffered some disrespect.

In parallel with the promotion of Rock n' Roll through Bill Haley, was that other rising star and exponent of rock music based on negro spirituals and country and western, non other than the icon of popular music for many years, Elvis Presley – who can forget that first hearing of 'Heartbreak Hotel' with that lilting, quivering voice throwing forth a blue's note of loss and loneliness? For a short time, our own singer Tommy Steele produced some original sounds in the mould of Rock n' Roll, but it was our 'equivalent' icon to Elvis, Cliff Richards who was to take our teenagers by storm in the late 1950's and continue his unique style of music to the present day.

It is interesting how the volatile oscillations of emotions in adolescence, lead sometimes to contrasting behaviours. I remember one Saturday making a fishing trip to Snailham, on my own, there I was 'lost' in the depths of the countryside with no sight of another human being, for several hours, just the natural world around me. Then at the end of the day, I could not wait to get home and go into the noise and hum of the town in the evening at the White Rock Pavilion, to hear a popular Rock n' Roll singer with a bright red wig, called Wee Willy Harris gyrating about the stage! The context with young people around me, intoxicated by the personality, and the music, was so different to that I was in a few hours earlier in my solitude on the marshes – but instead of a fish, I had now got an autograph!

The other form of popular music which came to the forefront from the mid-1950's, was not new, but a revival of music which evolved in the United States earlier in the 20th century, this was traditional jazz promoted by bands in the UK such as Chris Barber, Humphrey Lyttleton, Cy Laurie, Ken Colyer, Acker Bilk and many others. But the big bands were also still very popular such as Duke Ellington and Count Basie in the United States, and Ted Heath, Eric Delaney and the new sounds of Johnny Dankworth with Cleo Laine as his singer in the UK; in the States smaller groups such as the Dave Brubeck quartet were gaining in popularity. My mid-teen years coincided with these impacting popular music sounds and I had the opportunity to see and hear these great bands at the White Rock Pavilion in Hastings, on a

Sunday evening during the summer months in 1956.

The next year, 1957 when I was in the first year of the 6th form, I started going to the Hastings Traditional Jazz Club where the Dolphin Jazz Band was in residence. There was a predominance, but not exclusively, an audience comprised of Grammar School boys, High School girls and many of my earlier Secondary Modern School friends from the single sex school at Priory Road (yes, I had failed the 11 plus and with the support of my mother I had a second chance with the 12 plus and passed for the Grammar School). Several Secondary Modern School boys ended up being excellent jazz musicians, notably David Holt a guitarist who stayed in Hastings associated with various groups. Most of the Dolphin Jazz Band were ex-Grammar School boys with lead trumpeter, bearded Pete Treger, sprightly clarinetist Chris Watford, pensive and cool trombonist Brian Towers, very methodical drummer Alan Whitmore, bass player Johnie Griffiths who provided extra percussion by slapping the strings, and finally, banjo player Geoff Coates and occasional pianist John Collinson whose improvisations were certainly enhanced by the beer!

There were three main venues of different character for the jazz club which was open on Saturday evenings at either the railway hall overlooking Warrior Square railway station, or the Market Hall in George Street in the Old Town, and on a Friday, with great atmosphere, St. Clement's Caves on the West Hill; you could never get too hot here jiving with a temperature of a constant 10 degrees centigrade, but the air was dark and heavy with cigarette and pipe smoke (I am ashamed to admit I contributed to the latter, but I gave up 3 years ago after 52 years of pipe smoking), then there was the odour of beer. Later into the 1960's, some sessions were held at the old Bathing Pool at West St. Leonards. All venues had a bar, but additionally near the Market Hall there was the newly opened old Pump House and The Anchor for a wider range of drinks. The Market Hall was also the venue for the jazz club in the morning on Bank Holiday Mondays including Easter

Monday.

By the time I had become a regular attendee at the jazz club, I had got to master a few chords on a guitar I had bought with some money given me by my grandfather Booth, it cost less than £10 in those days. The guitar had a round sound hole and steel strings, a style used by folk singers; I bought the instrument in a little music shop in Cross Street leading off the junction of King's Road and London Road, St. Leonards. At this time there was yet another style of popular music evolving from traditional jazz clubs based on American folk music, this was skiffle introduced to the UK by Lonnie Donegan, the one time banjo and guitar player with Chris Barber's band. The number which hit the media and record shops was 'The Rock Island Line', a sound representing a steam rail train in the mid-west of the US through the penetrating twangy voice of Lonnie Donegan accompanied by rapid strummed guitars, a washboard struck with thimbles and a string bass. ' The Rock Island Line' was a great hit and skiffle groups sprung up all over Britain. Young men and some women of my age got together to form skiffle groups and I was destined to be one of them.

Five of us at the jazz club got together in 1957 to form the 1066 Skiffle Group. The main singers with guitars were Malcolm West and Chris Sayer, I was mostly instrumental guitar with some backing singing and we were accompanied by John Irvine on washboard and Terry Padgham on string bass, literally made from a length of strong string attached to the top of a ply wood tea chest acting as a sound chamber, and extended upwards to the end of a broom handle; a change in note was achieved by increasing or decreasing the tension on the string by a combination of part rocking the broom handle and shortening the string's length by pressing the string with one hand on the handle in different positions, the same principle as playing a proper string instrument.

From time to time other musicians joined us such as another pipe smoking enthusiast, Tony Hale who played a snare drum, and Phil Barker son of the band leader on the Pier. Our repertoire was a mixture of negro spirituals, railroad songs and more general American folk songs; later audiences started to ask for less traditional new pieces such as 'That'll be the Day' popularized by that other icon of pop music Buddy Holly who sadly was prematurely killed in a plane crash in America. We used to practice at Malcolm's house in Harrow Road on Saturday afternoons before relaxing in front of the TV to see and hear how our contemporaries were progressing on the 'Six-Five Special' show, introduced by Pete Murray. Incidently, in February 1957 the Dolphin Jazz Band was filmed in the Caves, to appear on the 'Six-Five Special' show which also included Big Bill Broonzy.

The year 1957-1958 was when the 1066 Skiffle Group took off. Apart from playing at the jazz club, we eventually had a regular Saturday night spot during the interval of the dances in the ballroom on Hastings Pier, on one of these occasions there was a screaming group of girls from Strawberry Hill, London who were so impressed with our performance that they rushed forward at the end of our session for us to sign our first autographs! From here we advanced to play at talent contests including 'Opportunity Knocks' with Hughie Green for Radio Luxembourg, unfortunately we just missed an opportunity here! More locally we won a contest on the stage of the Ritz cinema in Hastings and more memorably at the Aquarium Ballroom in Brighton, we came second out of a number of South Coast towns. I shall never forget that Monday evening on the return journey back to Hastings on the Southern Region electric train. We had a carriage to ourselves and near to midnight the group got together to play, what else but the 'Midnight Special', a rail road number – how appropriate to the sound and rhythm of a real train as it sped along the South Coast towards the Wealden shore in the dark; it is a pity that we did not have another audience, quite unique. This year of the launch of skiffle in Britain, led to an article in the Radio Times, on the story of skiffle. The closing words were,"A new musical form has been developed within our shores – bubbling with enthusiasm and joie de vivre. The 'decadent' youth of Britain is creating something worthwhile. Commercialised because of its popularity, criticized by the casual listener, it has still maintained its freshness. One thing is certain, as long as people want to be happy, skiffle will flourish". Perhaps people were not so happy because it did not flourish, but I do not think it was the reason I was soon to abandon this music.

The Christmas and New Year period of 1958 provided the opportunity for the 1066 Skiffle Group to play at parties and other functions in hotels and elsewhere and we got good money for our efforts. However, as 1958 progressed and 'A' levels were a year away, I found the draw of science and my future here hopefully with a university education, yet to come, my first priority and so I left the skiffle group. I obviously was not convinced that the 1066 Skiffle Group was going to progress to greater heights, although we were unaware at that time, that in other parts of the UK, other skiffle groups were going to evolve into something much more eye and ear catching such as the 'Beatles', and Cliff Richards arose to fame through a similar pathway. It is satisfying to look back to those days and be able to identify in a small way with those personalities who were to go on and put new sounds on the pop scene and change the course of popular music to the present day.

My interest in jazz did not wane; I bought a fine looking acoustic guitar, later amplified, and I continued to go to the jazz club for a few more years until I eventually left university, and Hastings for another life. I think my friend Barry was disappointed that I did not excel further on the guitar to become another Eric Clapton! When I went to university, my Grammar School friend Brian Newbery took over my acoustic guitar and I bought a Spanish 'Hofner Vienna' guitar, easier to travel with, and I continued some folk singing at university. Coincident with the arrival of Rock n' Roll and the revival of jazz, was the conversion of shop premises into coffee bars where young people could meet, talk and listen to the latest popular tune on that other import from America, the juke box. In Hastings there were two popular coffee bars, the 'Sombrero' in George Street and the 'Fiesta' in Trinity Street where a Gaggia coffee machine ejected expresso coffee into your cup and kept you alert for those youthful conversations.

The need to have some money in my pocket other than the small, but much appreciated amounts given to me as weekly pocket money by my father, took me to a newsagents at Mount Pleasant on the edge of town where I was offered a paper round 7 days a week for 17s 6d, around 90p in today's money, relatively much more is offered today. I started my paper round in 1957 at the start of my first year in the 6th form and continued for almost 2 years until I left the Grammar School in the hot summer of 1959. I used to leave home before 6.30 am and still on that war grade Raleigh bicycle I cycled down to the newsagents to collect my assignment of newspapers.

My round started at the bottom end of St. Helen's Park Road at the junction with Down's Road. The first hundred yards or so were 'made up' before it became a rough surfaced road typical of unadopted roads in the area of St. Helen's Wood. Most of the houses were Victorian or Edwardian and they often had long drives or many steps to negotiate with a heavy bag of newspapers. Several Grammar School masters lived in St. Helen's Park Road, notably Tom Cookson and his writer wife Catherine who had moved from the Hurst in Hoad's Wood Road to 'Loreto' a few years earlier. This house did not have a drive (the car went straight into a small garage from the road above the house), but I had to descend several steps through one garden gate to the house, and ascend by another flight of steps and back on to the road through another gate. On many mornings, Catherine Cookson would take a copy of the Daily Telegraph from me and we would have a short chat while Simon the cream labrador retriever would excitedly sniff around my feet. Further up St. Helen's Park Road was another, but older larger, Victorian house called 'Oaklands' where I delivered newspapers. Here, many years earlier, lived the author Warwick Deeping (1877-1950) who, while a medical student was staying at 'Oaklands' his father's house. Warwick Deeping gave up being a medical practioner soon after qualifying, to become a popular author in the 1920's; his best selling novel was 'Sorrell and Son', and I have a copy of another of his novels, 'Suvla John'. Warwick Deeping said in a letter of his childhood that, "This Sussex landscape seems miraculous".

Sunday was the worst day delivering newspapers, due to the fact that even in the 1950's the newspapers were getting heavier at the weekends, so much so that the manager of the newsagents would drop off another load of papers under a hedge for me, half way on the route so that I could complete my round in Oakwood Close. The Close was a post war development of houses and bungalows on the fields where I went black-berrying with my mother in the 1940's. My paper round on Sunday finished with deliveries to a few houses in Langham Road followed by a short journey back home. Also on a Sunday after this hour plus expenditure of energy first thing in the morning, the rest of the day would often be taken up with a fishing trip and getting there by bicycle. Another aspect about a 7 day paper round lasting about an hour, was that I did the round on 6 school days because the Grammar School was open on Saturday morning, but closed on Wednesday afternoon as mentioned earlier. Every school day was very tight on time getting the paper round finished, followed by a quick breakfast and back on the bicycle to school by 8.50 am, but one Saturday morning, a busy paper round day collecting the money from customers, I was slightly late for school and a master outside the morning assembly said to me, *"Quick Booth, get on the stage your name is being read out for you to be sworn in as a new prefect!"*, an embarrassing moment, but I just made it on to the stage in front of the masters and pupils so that I could remain a 'responsible' candidate for election to prefect status.

The Christmas of 1958 when I was well into my paper round, and had got to know a number of customers who paid me at the door on Saturday mornings, provided me with a substantial Christmas box of tips; I received over £5, more than 5 weeks of paper round wages. I put this money to good use and bought a navy duffle coat which kept me warm and dry for paper rounds and generally worn during the winter months. Since my paper round days, at least three daily newspapers have gone out of production, they are the News Chronicle, Reynolds News and the Sunday Pictorial; others like The Sun and Daily Star have come into being on a 'lighter note'.

One final episode has to be recalled for my days on that black war grade Raleigh, these were trips unrelated to fishing, just cycle rides for exercise and exploring the Weald and beyond. Back to my final 'O' level years of 1957. During the summer term when the long warm evenings of late May and June arrived, after returning home from school, having a traditional tea and completing my home work, I would set off on my bicycle in a northerly direction for an evening's ride to stretch my muscles and absorb the musky odours of the Wealden lanes and woods. Journeys using my father's pre-war Ordnance Survey map of East Sussex and Kent would take me to destinations as far away as Goudhurst that village high on the mid-Weald, 21 miles from Hastings and returning with a detour south to the outskirts of Bexhill before descending to the coastal A259 road back to the promenade of Hastings and home.

The longest trip I ever made on the old bike, was a whole day during the school holidays in the summer of 1957. Leaving Hoad's Wood Road about 8.30 am, my route took me via Icklesham to Rye on the A259, then along the road running parallel with the Military Canal skirting the edge of Romney Marsh to Appledore, Woodchurch and Ashford, and then on the main road to Canterbury via Wye along the valley of the River Stour. I arrived in Canterbury, 45 miles from Hastings, by late morning for refreshments and a visit to the magnificent Cathedral to see the site of the murder of Thomas Becket and the tomb of the

Black Prince. In addition, I had the unexpected opportunity to see the eccentric Red Dean (with Communist sympathies) of Canterbury, Dr Hewlett Johnson with long white hair – he walked by me in the central aisle. From Canterbury, I continued along the main road for another 15 miles to Margate in time for lunch and a well-earned ice cream on the sands.

Up to now, the weather had been fine, but on the return journey back to Hastings the wind increased from the south west, which meant the cyclist's nightmare, a head wind all the way home. The extra energy needed for the journey was challenged by the fact that my route took me over the North Downs with its steep hills and valleys and along the coast via Deal, Dover, Folkestone to Hythe; it was here down in the flat country and across Romney Marsh that I experienced the full force of the wind. After Rye, there was the climb back up the Wealden hills by an alternative route through Pett village to the White Hart Inn on the brow of the hill above Guestling and just before Ore village; it was now 8.30 pm, exactly 12 hours from when I started my excursion. I was exhausted; remember the war grade Raleigh had no gears, it was heavy and I had just completed 120 miles over a hilly and windy landscape! I relaxed with a packet of crisps and a non alcoholic drink (I was still only 17), as I sat on a bench outside the White Hart and looked across the countryside, I had just 'conquered', I felt I had just climbed the bean stalk. Needless to say that war grade bicycle went to the scrap heap, it, also exhausted a few years later when I went to university, it had served a good life.

View from the West Hill towards the Harbour and fishing boats (top left)

with the boating lake in mid-view (1961).

View from the West Hill over the 'new town'

with the Central Cricket Ground in mid-view (1961).

The Dolphin Jazz Band at the Railway Hall in the mid-1950's.

Left to right – Brian Towers, John Griffiths, Pete Treger,

Alan Whitmore, Chris Watford, Johnnie Collinson.

The '1066' Skiffle Group on the Pier in 1958.

Left to right – Terry Padgham, Malcolm West, Chris Sayer, Derek Booth, John Irvine.

126

Capturing the atmosphere of the jazz club

in St.Clement's Caves during the 1950's.

©   Brian Newbery

The second and last house 'Loreto' of Tom and Catherine Cookson

in Hastings, at St. Helen's Park Road. The author as a 6th form pupil,

delivered newspapers to the Cooksons at the white door (centre of picture).

©   Piers Dudgeon

10. "Tickets Please"

I have now reached the last chapter of my childhood spent in Hastings as 'Boy of the Wealden Shore', and appropriately it was an experience closely associated with or near the sea shore. This was as a deck chair attendant, a transition occupation between leaving school, Hastings and indeed later, university before entering a career complementing my education and interests while living in other regions of the UK.

I left the Hastings Grammar School at the end of the summer term in 1959 when I was 19 years old, those who had passed the 11 plus and had stayed on at school for their 'A' levels, were on average a year younger than me when they left the Grammar School unless they stayed on a third year in the 6th form to take a state scholarship examination. Having left school, I needed to earn a living for the next few months during which time I was waiting for that piece of paper in the post indicating that I had achieved successful 'A' level results to go to university. Boys in my position often worked as conductors on the buses or became deck chair attendants, and some boys also came from public schools. These opportunities arose to earn reasonable money with commission because extra staff were needed in these occupations, as tourists flocked into the town during the summer with Hastings being then still a popular seaside resort; these were the days before many people went on an aeroplane to take a holiday in various parts of the world to find more assured sunshine.

I was fortunate that there was a vacancy on the deck chairs, so I got the job as a regular deck chair attendant employed by the Hastings Borough Council in July, and this lasted until early September after the August Bank Holiday. This summer occupation was repeated for the next 3 years because I got a good clutch of 'A' levels and went to the University of Hull in East Yorkshire to read for an honours degree in zoology. Yorkshire was a county I had got to like because I had spent holidays with my parents in York City, staying with an army friend of my father and his wife earlier in the 1950's, and had visited a number of places of scenic and historic interest in the county. I felt that Hull and the coast of the East Riding was the 'big brother' in the fishing industry by comparison with Hastings, but with its bracing climate in some ways it was 'home from home'.

Before reflecting on particular experiences on the deck chairs, it is useful to outline the staff structure and pitches where the deck chairs were placed; I will refer to the permanent staff simply by their initials. The staff office was under the promenade opposite Warrior Square and after you emerged from Bottle Alley walking in a westerly direction. The person in charge was superintendent Mr. R, a stocky, bald headed man, probably around 50 years old at the most, wearing black trousers, white shirt, black tie and robust black framed glasses. Mr. R. was a jovial character always telling amusing tales, some rather crude, but he was also a hard driver accepting no nonsense from his staff, including the casual staff like me. Beneath him in the management peck order was the senior inspector J.N., a large older man probably at least 60 years old who said little and always wore the full uniform of a black suit, white shirt and black tie, and white peak hat even on the hottest days. J.N. would amble along the promenade and go to the beach with his own reel of tickets and clippers to issue as a 'fill in' if the general attendant had overlooked, or not yet reached the customers – just checking up on the lower rank attendant's thoroughness! Then there were two other younger inspectors K.P. and B.B. These inspectors were in their 40's and also wore the full formal uniform and were the main managers on the beat.

General attendants like me, only had to wear a light weight brown jacket supplied with the job and sometimes a white peak hat was available, but not compulsory. However, I did wear a white peak hat for awhile and because the front of the hat turned upwards, I was called 'Rommel' after the German senior officer in the War, a rather derogatory comparison I think, but I was not offended. Each day the assignment of pitches was reviewed. The temporary staff like me probably had the widest exposure to different pitches, whereas some of the older permanent staff seemed to prefer to remain on the same pitch which I suppose for various reasons, they had become attached to.

The pitches themselves were divided into three zones. The largest zone was the beach and promenade extending about 3 miles from Rock-a-Nore to the Bathing Pool at St. Leonards. No.1 pitch was Rock-a-Nore to the Harbour. This included the beach where the fishing boats are drawn up on the beach by cables (this simple way of boats coming to land, goes back to Saxon days over 1000 years ago), and the catch off-loaded for the Fish Market. These boats are also a favourite subject for watercolour artists. One such person was the Rev. Denbigh Hilton, a Unitarian minister who with his wife Muriel lived opposite my parents' house in Hoad's Wood Road; the Unitarian Church is in South Terrace. Muriel published several small books of poems and short stories – an occurring theme was the pleasure of the simple things in life; the stories included every day events, with some about two school girls living nearby who I knew, who would visit Muriel for tea or cookery lessons (Muriel and Denbigh had no children). Muriel was also a close friend of that other authoress who used to live in Hoad's Wood Road, Catherine Cookson, Catherine used to give talks on her writing to the Literary Society which Muriel founded at her church. Denbigh and Muriel died in the same decade as Catherine and Tom Cookson, the 1990's. I shall never forget the image of Denbigh leaving his house – distinguished with long wavy hair, horn-rimmed glasses, weathered and kind face, and wearing an unbuttoned coat as he hurried along the road swinging his brief case, to catch the bus into town. Likewise, Muriel was an upright, fine featured woman with an angelic smile and dark hair tightly drawn into a bun – both Denbigh and Muriel truly reflected their vocation in life.

No 2 pitch covered the area from the Harbour to the boating lake. No.3 pitch was opposite the old De Luxe cinema and the Castle, followed by pitches No.4 and 5 opposite the Queen's Hotel (it is here where the Priory stream runs out on to the beach). No.6 pitch was opposite one of Hastings prestigious national features, the indoor swimming baths with heated salt water direct from the sea, (now sadly gone but very much in use still in the 1960's). The steepest beach down from the promenade with a long flight of steps was No.7 pitch followed by No.8 pitch next to the Pier where pedal boats could be hired. To the west of the Pier and along Bottle Alley were pitches No. 9 and 10. West of here were pitches No.11 and 12 covering the area from Warrior Square to Marine Court. The last two pitches were No.13 opposite the Royal Victoria Hotel and finally from here to the Bathing Pool pitch No.14. In my 4 years on the deck chairs, I worked all the beach pitches.

The second zone was the inland pitches. Nearest to the sea front was the White Rock Gardens with its model village and floral clock, and deck chairs around the bowling green. A regular occupant of one of these chairs was a town character, 'Boag' – an old Russian soldier with Christ-like hair and long beard; he wore a long Khaki overcoat. Boag's belongings seemed to be confined to an old sack which he threw over his shoulder as he walked around the town – a typical tramp. But he was not detached from people, he could be seen talking to all sorts of people and they respected him; a most kindly and soft spoken man. I witnessed this when I reluctantly approached him with my ticket machine – I would not have charged him for his chair. But Boag insisted, he was going to pay for his canvas seat watching the bowls like everyone else, his medals sparkling in the afternoon sun .

Many of the chairs here were old and 'preserved' with several coats of dark brown paint. These old chairs were not deck chairs but folding up-right chairs and the many joints contributed to their fragility and broke easily – they became known by the unfortunate name of 'cripple fingers'. I witnessed some nasty accidents with people sitting in these chairs and putting their fingers in the frame before the weight of their body produced a scissor effect as the frame broke on their fingers. Fortunately these chairs were soon replaced by more modern designs.

The other inland zone was Alexandra Park by the band stand. I worked both these inland pitches and they were a welcome change, particularly in the Park to get away from trudging the hard and hot (or wet and windy) promenade and beaches. Apart from the relative green and cool of the Park, it made a pleasant, relaxing Sunday afternoon issuing the chair tickets for those listening to the band, an experience I could share with them. Furthermore, with the Park tea room nearby, I could take quiet refreshment here and still hear the music as it wafted through the open doors of the tea room.

The third zone was back to the promenade, or rather the Pier extension owned by the Borough Council which linked the promenade to the main Pier owned by a private company. I worked this pitch, on a Wednesday evening when a band played on the band stand situated in the centre of the extension. This in turn was surrounded by two covered pavilions with deck chairs.. At each end of these pavilions was a small room with a domed roof and on each dome was a flag pole. The resident deck chair attendant for the Pier extension during the day was a small cheery man, getting on in years, called B.C. When I arrived in the evening to take over from B.C., his first task was to instruct me on how to attach, and raise the flag on each of the four flag poles; it took awhile to work out the knots on the ropes and the pulley system! Liking the music emanating from the band stand, provided me with another relaxing working experience in the cool of the evening, watching the holiday makers and residents go by on the promenade in the direction of the sunset and me being paid for it!

A typical working day would be to report to the office by 9.00 am and find out which pitch you would be on and then to collect your ticket machine, tickets and leather money bag with a float of small change. The first year or two, the ticket machines were the really old punch types, the nickel - silver finish had now worn away to expose the brass underneath and you carried a separate roll of coloured tickets, a different colour for different half day sessions. Later, the ticket machines took white rolls of paper and the price, time and date were printed on the paper to be torn off and given to the customer. At about the same time or earlier, the buses adopted a similar ticket machine.

People would be arriving at the promenade or beach from around 9.30 am on a fine day. I put a line of deck chairs out along the promenade by the railings overlooking the beach; the chairs came from large stacks placed at intervals along the promenade by the iron steps that led down to the beach. Those people going on to the beach collected their own chairs from the stacks. As the morning progressed I would walk round the pitch to issue tickets and if unsure whether I had approached everyone, I would call out *"Any more tickets please?"* I hoped as the beach became more crowded that those who had not yet paid for their deck chairs, would be forthcoming with their coins. Mid - morning after this initial collection, those attendants working the promenade and beaches would all walk to the office to hand in the money and take a coffee break in one of the many cafes along the promenade, this meant a lot of walking in addition to that done on the beaches, if your pitch was at the extreme ends of the town.

At lunch time, I either had a bite to eat in a cafe or pub with other deck chair attendants, or went home on the bus for lunch, however the latter did not give me much time. As a consequence of this in my first year on the chairs, I had an embarrassing experience. I was unintentionally late back to the beach from home whereupon the superintendent Mr. R. and an inspector were already walking over my pitch which happened to be near the office, issuing tickets for the afternoon session. My excuse was that people were either on the beach all day, or had come down for the afternoon, either way I would cover all at 2.30 pm as I would at 2.00 pm, probably more, but my logic was not accepted – the arrogance of my youth was not in my favour and I was threatened with the loss of my job if it happened again, of course it never did! I think this incident in some ways reflected the discipline in society at that time, it seemed like school again with both schoolmasters and deck chair managers, frequently men who had experienced the discipline of the armed forces during the War.

The afternoon – evening session followed the same pattern as the morning, taking the money back to the office in the late afternoon associated with a refreshment break with the exception that there was no obligation on behalf of the customers to return the deck chairs to the stacks on the promenade. This happened after I left in 1962 when a deposit system was adopted and the attendants had less walking to do; the attendants issued the chairs and received a deposit from the customers who later returned the chairs to the promenade and received back their deposit from the attendant.. But for me at the end of a long, often hot day, I had to walk round the beach and collect all those vacated chairs which were the majority – 5 deck chairs on one shoulder and 4 carried over the other arm, up and down the beach until all were collected in and neatly stacked on the promenade, and covered with a tarpaulin; this often took me into the evening on a busy day; we certainly earned our money. How many of our students do this sort of hard manual work today to earn their living when not studying? The girls who had been at the High School and were also students wanting to earn some money, frequently worked in the large number of cafes and restaurants in the town, and if near the beach they might provide the young deck chair attendants with refreshments, a quick chat and perhaps 'a date' would arise for the weekend!

I have reviewed a general working day on the deck chairs, but what made the job interesting were the annual events in Hastings, often typical for a seaside resort and the chance meeting with so many different people from the public and the anecdotes arising from these encounters. One of the first events in the summer was the National Town Criers' Competition when town criers from all over Britain came to Hastings promenade to compete for who had the loudest and clearest voice and delivered the most appealing message. The deck chair attendants with the help of the inspectors set out hundreds of deck chairs along the promenade in the morning for the event later in the day. Another similar placing of deck chairs along the promenade was for the Hastings Carnival procession.

The greatest drama I can recall was the Sunday Mirror talent contest held on the extensive flat beach (which had been building up over decades as shingle was carried by the west to east Channel currents) opposite the De Luxe cinema. One Sunday morning the day of the talent show, a large lorry arrived with the stage. The lorry had to be driven on to the beach over duck boards, but these obviously were not strong enough, they broke, and the lorry sank into the shingle - marooned. Panic set in as time was running out for getting the stage assembled for the day's event. Somehow through improvising with discarded planks and pieces of corrugated iron from the nearby fishing boat area, and 'all hands on deck' including us deck chair attendants, the lorry was on the move again and positioned for the stage to be assembled on board. Eventually the show got under way by the afternoon and the mostly young ladies in their swimming costumes coyly filed by on the stage, each hoping they would be the winner – of course the young deck chair attendants had decided who should be No.1!

Other events were not formalized, they were on the job experiences, I recall a few. A sociologist or psychologist would have had plenty of observations on human behaviour and its demographic distribution to ponder on, along the 3 mile promenade and beaches at Hastings and St. Leonards. Deck chair pitches No.1 to 3 at the Old Town end was where the East-Enders from London would arrive at the weekend in their red, London double decker buses parked on the nearby coach park by the Fish Market. Whole families and friends would 'fall out' of these poorly ventilated modes of transport, obviously a cheap trip, but unsuitable for the 65 mile journey from London, particularly on a hot day. These people would stagger, travel worn, to the nearest fish and chip bars and cafes, and wash their greasy meal down with a pint of two in one of the many public houses an easy walking distance away.

By early afternoon, these London visitors well fed and watered, made their way on to the beach and the bigger the group, the bigger the amphitheatre of deck chairs they assembled – then I arrived with ticket machine at the ready to make a focused collection of money. You can imagine the comments I received from this happy crowd, such as, *"Is there a discount mate for all us lot?"* What else would you expect from these shrewd East-Enders? But it was the settling into the chairs that was amusing, these city dwellers, particularly the older ones, did not know how much clothing to take off and how to do this sitting in the 'protection' of a deck chair? Usually it was just shirts off for the men and bras exposed for the women, the beginnings of a theme for a saucy postcard. There was also the inevitable paper hat or knotted handkerchief on the bald heads of men to protect the scalp from the intense seaside sun and breeze. Another comment which I regularly received, was *"What do you do in the winter mate?"* Of course the permanent deck chair staff cleaned and repaired chairs in the store area by the office in the winter, but I had to be honest and say I was a university student, however these East-Enders could not understand why I would ever want to do such a lowly job as a deck chair attendant. For me doing this job, apart from the money, was the good air, physical exercise and meeting a variety of people enjoying a day out at the seaside – all part of being educated into the world, not just pursuing a narrow academic field, indeed a universal education not just a university education.

Before leaving the old town area of Hastings and being a deck chair attendant here, I had the unique experience of bridging the gap between academia and the situation I was in as a deck chair attendant in my home town. I was checking between the moored up fishing boats on pitch No.1 to see whether anyone had dragged a chair to shelter from the shore wind, when, there was the vice president, a woman, of the student's union at Hull University accompanied by a post graduate student a man in the zoology department at Hull, indeed a small world as these 'Hullarians' were not local people to Hastings.

The centre of town pitches from opposite the Queen's Hotel to Marine Court, were the most cosmopolitan of the pitches. Here was where most families, individuals, young people including the many foreign students studying English at the language schools, came down to relax on the beach; my parents and I, and later my sister and brother also went on these pitches particularly to the west of the pier. Aspects which made the centre area of the beach and promenade most popular were the proximity to the shops, refreshments (ice cream bars), public houses, toilets, etc. Furthermore, there was the minimum of shingle and more sand for shrimping with nets at low tide with the Castle rocks and pools of shore life exposed, and particularly opposite the indoor swimming baths on pitch No.7 where the sand almost came up to the steep promenade wall; this was due to the scouring of the shingle from this small stretch of the coast where there was a slight indent in the shore line and the shingle then deposited as referred to earlier, by the Channel current further east towards the Harbour.

It was at this centre area of the beach, on pitch No.6 that I was involved in a unique and dramatic event early one afternoon on returning from my lunch break, and just about to start issuing the tickets for the afternoon session. The weather was very calm, sultry, slightly foggy and it was high tide, and therefore everyone was concentrated on a very narrow area of beach between the water's edge and the promenade. These conditions were ideal for a show often given by 'Biddy the Tubman' who dressed in a fisherman's blue jersey, rolled up trousers, bare footed and wearing a top hat, would stand astride a wooden tub and with a paddle, spin round faster and faster until he fell into the sea. Floating on the water was just the tub, paddle and top hat, then to everyone's relief Biddy surfaced to do a show another day; Biddy had been doing this show since before the First World War, but not this afternoon. All of a sudden, without warning, the quiet lapping of the small waves as they gently broke on the beach magnified into a large surge of water which rushed up the remaining beach – people grabbed their belongings, children were screaming and there were a number of belongings, floating in the water, mostly beach balls; there were also a number of deck chairs dislodged from the shingle floating around to add to the chaos. My first action was to help people gather their belongings together and concern myself with the deck chairs later. After a few minutes, with no repeat of the sea's unexpected behaviour, things got back to more or less normal. The cause of this phenomenon was a sudden drop in air pressure out to sea giving rise to what is known as a 'fog swell'; I never witnessed this again, thank goodness.

West of Marine Court and the Sun Lounge was pitch No.13 opposite the Royal Victoria Hotel, this part of the promenade attracted the more affluent people. They were either visitors staying at the Royal Victoria Hotel, other hotels or up-market guest houses in West St. Leonards, or who had retired to the area, perhaps staying in similar accommodation. These would be your ex-military officers, bank managers and civil servants with their lean brown bodies and thin moustaches. When I approached such people sitting in a Hastings Borough Council deck chair (borough council ownership revealed by the burnt on initials HBC on the side of the chair), they would hold up a green card and authoritatively say *"Season!"*, no other qualification while they continued to stare out to sea, or be immersed in the pages of 'The

Times' or an Agatha Christie plot. 'Season' of course was a season ticket for a deck chair and I collected no money or issued a ticket to the customer on this occasion.

Being at the seaside when gales are blowing and the rain stings your face during the summer months, is not what most people go to the coast for as a leisure break, but it happens all too frequently in our climate. I recall one such August Bank Holiday Monday when I was on duty on the stretch of beach by Bottle Alley. Here there are bastions, protrusions of the promenade, where on the lower promenade of Bottle Alley there were shutters which were pulled round in steel runners by the deck chair attendant, these shutters were situated towards the outside of the bastion; and gave immediate and welcomed protection from the elements. Within this confined area of the bastion, those still persuaded to stay on the promenade were crammed together in deck chairs making the best of a miserable day with an ice cream bought from the convenient kiosk nearby.

My final story reflects how some people's lives were tragically altered by the Second World War which had only finished 15 years earlier. During the morning, a bronzed, medium height, balding man with a scant beard, perhaps a little older than my father in his 50's, used to arrive on pitch No.9 just west of the Pier. This man would spread out a large brown check blanket on the beach and settle down to read a paper back. As this was a regular occurrence, I got into conversation with this apparent vagrant and found out that his name was Steve. When Steve spoke it was evident that he was an educated man and this was in keeping with the sad story he was willing to tell me about his life. Steve had been a classics master at St. Paul's School in London, but during the War his wife and one or more of his children had been killed in a bombing raid on London. This traumatic event involving the loss of the core and purpose of his life, had turned Steve into a part vagrant, living and sleeping rough on the South Coast in the summer, but returning to London for work and accommodation in the winter. Deck chair attendants had one day off a week. On one of these days, Steve invited me and another deck chair attendant, ex-Hastings Grammar School boy George Noakes to his coastal home on the Wealden shore, a cave on the cliffs at Ecclesbourne glen. George and I bought Steve and ourselves some food and we took it in turns to carry Steve's blanket and books back from the beach to his temporary home retreat on the cliffs. When we arrived at the small recess looking out to sea, George and I had our picnic with Steve and we learned more about this unfortunate man's life. This whole experience was so moving and never to be forgotten.

I often wonder what happened to Steve, if alive today I am sure he would be well over 100 years old, an almost lost generation. For me, I was still young with hopefully many years ahead of me to make something of life, what adventures would I encounter? I finally left Hastings and my parents' home in Hoad's Wood Road as 'Boy of the Wealden Shore' for another life in August 1962; I was only going to return from time to time to visit my relatives with my own family. In 2002 my mother died, my father had died 3 years earlier, I could no longer share any further experiences of this life with them and the house in Hoad's Wood Road was soon sold after being the family home for 61 years.

The author at the end of a hard day's work where the beach

was furthest from the promenade.

A more tranquil pitch (apart from the jet aircraft!)

at White Rock bowling green.

Fishing boats moored up on the beach between the Harbour

and Rock-a-Nore (deck chair pitch No.1).

(photograph of watercolour painting by the Rev. Denbigh Hilton,

provided as a gift to the author's family)

'East-Enders' relaxing in a deck chair after a hot

bus journey from London.

11. Beyond the Wealden Shore

'Boy of the Wealden Shore' grew up, became a man, and left Hastings because opportunities in the town after university in the 1960's were limited. I left Hull University in the summer of 1962; studying in the library of Philip Larkin the university librarian and distinguished poet, I had got my special honours degree in zoology. Doug Brightmore my biology master at the Grammar School, invited me to become his assistant biology master at the school which was now in a new building with its sports' fields off St. Helen's Road, later to become the William Parker Comprehensive School. A few years earlier when I was a pupil at the Grammar School, to think then that one day I would have the opportunity to become one of the masters at the school, would have been beyond my wildest dreams. But now, I had to decline the offer, I could not go back to the 'other side of the teacher's desk', I had moved on to finding out new knowledge to further our understanding of fertility problems. (By a strange coincidence, the person who did get the teaching post with Doug, was a contemporary zoology graduate from Hull University, Eddie Reader who I knew, but I had nothing to do directly with promoting his cause).

The employment which introduced me to human fertility problems, was being offered a research assistant post in the Endocrine Laboratories of the Obstetric Research Unit of University College Hospital Medical School (UCHMS), London. The work in these laboratories was concerned with diagnosing infertility through examining sperm quality and hormonal imbalances. I was fortunate to obtain the position as a research assistant at UCHMS because it followed on from my degree specialisms in comparative endocrinology and physiology. (About 2 months had elapsed after leaving Hull and during a day off from the deck chairs, I went into the library extension in Hastings and looked at the 'New Scientist' magazine for the availability of scientific posts – there was the employment for me – the post at UCHMS! After travelling to London for an interview, I was offered the job). Although London was not my first choice of a place to live and work, I had been offered an employment which suited my interests, qualifications and opportunity to progress in a career.

The Endocrine Laboratories were dominated by women scientists and technicians (perhaps it was the emphasis of work on women's infertility, and in an obstetric research unit?). But there was one man, David Richardson working on the preservation of human semen in an adjacent laboratory who eventually became my best man when I married Judith Harrison, a Hull graduate in history, in December 1963. Our marriage took place at the Methodist Church in Daventry where Judith's father, the minister, officiated. The venue of our honeymoon sounds romantic in context, it was Castle Godwyn, a large Victorian house reached by a track through woodland in the hamlet of Adam and Eve Paradise, near Stroud in Gloucestershire, but the weather on arrival was so foggy, the taxi driver had difficulty in locating the entrance. The house had a large hall way with a Christmas tree competing with the staircase for access to a surrounding gallery to the bedrooms; Judith and I had the house to ourselves with a large log fire in the lounge and being looked after by two embarrassed girl students while the owner went away to Norfolk!

One of the technicians working on the bench with me, was Diana King (nee Lawson), sister of Nigel Lawson who later became the Chancellor of the Exchequer in Margaret Thatcher's Conservative government; Nigel Lawson's daughter Nigella, a mere toddler when I was working in the laboratories with her aunt Diana, was later to become the celebrity cook. Diana was very helpful in introducing me to various laboratory techniques, she approached chemical methods like a cook dealing with recipes. To illustrate this, Diana used a glass laboratory separating funnel in her kitchen to separate fat from stock, the fat stayed at the top of the conical funnel while the water phase was run off the bottom through a tap; in the laboratory of course, this equipment was used for separating fatty substances including steroid hormones, extracted into an organic solvent from a water phase, perhaps urine or blood. There seems to be a 'culinary gene' inherited at least on the female side of the Lawson family!

During my 3 years in London, I lived in a number of different areas of the metropolis. Until I got married to Judith, my first accommodation was in a bedsitting room with George Noakes my ex-Grammar School friend who was about to start a degree course in French at Queen Mary College. The accommodation was at Stamford Hill, not far from the Tottenham Hotspur's football stadium which was convenient for George who was a football enthusiast. As the underground was not far away from the accommodation, I usually took this into the City, but occasionally I cycled to UCHMS along the busy roads on my roadster-sports Raleigh 'Blue Streak' bicycle which I bought when I was at Hull University. After Stamford Hill, George and I moved into a furnished self catering flat in an Edwardian mansion on Holloway Road – the A1 road was in front of the property, the Piccadilly underground line ran underneath, and the main line railway from King's Cross to the North passed by the western side of the flat; this resulted in some considerable vibration within the building! However, one bonus was seeing the classic steam train with its engine the 'Flying Scotsman' pass by our window when it was a regular service to Edinburgh and steam engines were still in operation; this was in 1962-'63. It was while I was at this accommodation that my bicycle was stolen, I naively left it in a yard at the back of the property over the Spring Bank Holiday and although locked and covered it was obviously taken *in toto*. By this time Judith and I were cultivating our relationship and she was living in furnished accommodation at Golder's Green – it was also the arctic winter of the recent decades and I had some rather difficult cycling journeys across north London from Golder's Green to Holloway Road. Eventually the icy winter turned to spring and Judith moved to Fellows Road in Belsize Park; soon after this I followed to the same area, to Primrose Gardens to a bedsitting room on my own. This location enabled me to have a much shorter cycle journey into work (I now had an old bicycle once belonging to Judith's brother), with the alternative transport of the underground, or on a fine day, a walk through Regent's Park which was the main part of London between Primrose Gardens and UCHMS.

By the end of 1963, as mentioned earlier, Judith and I got married, after which we moved to an unfurnished flat on the top floor of a Victorian house in Blackheath, south east London. Blackheath like Belsize Park which was not far from Hampstead Heath, were once villages outside London, but had now become absorbed into the great metropolis, at the same time, maintaining a certain village character with green spaces and trees. Blackheath was convenient for Judith's teaching post as a history teacher after she had obtained her post graduate diploma in education at the Institute of Education at London University; the post was at Buller's Wood, a technical high school near Bromley. Judith's journey to the school was mainly by the Southern Region railway line (which eventually terminated at Hastings). As for me, I took the main line train from Blackheath to Charing Cross, followed by the underground or a walk to UCHMS. I also, on a few occasions, cycled down off the Heath into Greenwich, through Deptford and Bermondsey to Tower Bridge, by St. Paul's Cathedral, along Fleet Street and on to UCHMS. Just before Judith and I left London for Cambridge, I bought a second hand Triumph 'Tina' scooter from a teacher friend of Judith which made me a free agent from the crowds on the trains, once I got the engine to start - a sluggish two-stroke! But, this vehicle got me to Cambridge on the day we left Blackheath and I eventually passed my motorcycle test on this unreliable mode of transport with no manual gears, which then qualified me to ride the largest motorcycle on the planet or a three-wheeler car.

Before leaving commentary on my time in London, there was one unique and impressive event that my wife Judith and I witnessed, that was the funeral of the great statesman, Winston Churchill in January 1965. It was a typical cold and overcast winter's day. We stood on the pavement in Fleet Street, not far from St. Paul's Cathedral where the funeral service was held, and we had a good view of the procession; shop workers and some people working in offices on a Saturday morning, were on the door steps or peering out of windows to see this once in a life time event. After the service in St. Paul's, and having waited outside during this time, we then walked briskly through the back streets (still showing the aftermath of the War with bomb damaged buildings), and arrived at London Bridge to see Churchill's coffin being transferred from a gun carriage to a boat at the Tower of London. Within a short time, we leaned over the bridge to see the coffin pass under the Bridge, on its way up the Thames to Waterloo Station (as part of the final journey to Bladon churchyard near the home of his ancestors, at Blenheim Palace). Then an amazing spectacle occurred, all the cranes situated along the wharfs (London was still an active port), were lowered as a gesture of respect as the boat with the coffin continued towards the railway station.

After the 3 years as a research assistant at UCHMS, the move to Cambridge was where I was going to be for the rest of my life until the present day. Reasons for moving to Cambridge were two fold. First, Judith and I, did not want to bring up a family in the London area, also the price of property was high. Secondly, I had got to know scientists working in my field, in Cambridge, and I wanted to carry out research with animals for more fundamental studies on reproduction than could be done on our own species, I

147

suppose this was the influence of having studied zoology. Fortunately there was a post at the Animal Research Station in Cambridge for me to establish, and apply work on hormone analysis to research projects on reproduction in laboratory and farm animals.

During my years of research at the Animal Research Station in Cambridge supported by the then Agricultural Research Council, my main contributions were to increasing our understanding of reproduction and behaviour in the pig with particular reference to hormones and the sense of smell (olfaction). The male pig or boar emits a scent (pheromone) in its saliva; this 'after shave' excites the sow to mate as well as stimulating the ovaries to produce eggs, the same odour can give pig meat an unpleasant taint. The highlight of my work was discovering a particular protein which carries the pheromone, a musky steroid into the saliva. During the course of my work, I became a member of the Institute (now Society) of Biology, and awarded a PhD for some of the work; I finally reached the grade of principal scientific officer. The views from the Animal Research Station were in total contrast to those from the windows of the Obstetric Unit in London. In London the view was the new Post Office tower being erected, whereas from the laboratory at the Research Station were fields with sheep and cattle, redwings and fieldfares in winter; looking west towards brilliant sunsets over the American cemetery at Madingley Rise, I could hear the distinctive call of the little owl in the willows by the stream at the bottom of the fields, even in the middle of the day

Family life in Cambridge over the last 45 years, more than twice the time I spent as a child in Hastings, has likewise provided many treasured experiences and memories; the exception being the sad loss of our eldest child Amanda who died of leukaemia at 4 years of age, mentioned earlier. But before Judith and I started a family, Judith worked as an educational advisor for the Advisory Centre for Education (ACE) in Cambridge, which published 'Where', the sister magazine to 'Which' at that time. After Amanda died, Judith compiled a book 'Grants for Higher Education' for ACE, published by Barrie & Jenkins in 1973. Our other two daughters Rebecca and Catherine attended the local Milton primary school, a Church of England foundation in 1836, but housed on a new site in 1959. Both girls subsequently went to Impington Village College, the first of a number of village colleges established in Cambridgeshire for secondary and adult education before becoming comprehensive schools. Impington Village College was opened in 1939 and was designed by the notable architects Maxwell Fry and Walter Gropius whose product was a typical inter war building with straight dimensions and little frills. Our two grandsons have followed the same educational pathway. With Rebecca and Catherine at school, Judith taught students History for many years as a part-time tutor at Sixth Form Colleges in Cambridge.

At home, I spent my time maintaining our two successive cottages and attending to the gardens; often part of my annual leave was used for this purpose. The remainder of leave from the laboratory was taken as family holidays, these were modest but often adventurous driving to camp sites in the UK or in France. On one occasion, I drove Judith and youngest daughter Catherine to Leningrad (now St.Petersberg) via ferries to Sweden and Finland, but not camping - there were some rather nervous moments! On reaching retirement, these self reliant holidays were gradually replaced by coach tours to Europe. When I was in research, I also had the opportunity to go abroad to scientific meetings as well as attending meetings back in the UK.

My work continued into the 1990's when due to government cuts in funding for research, I took early retirement. In 2008, Professor 'Twink' Allen CBE, Professor of Equine Reproduction at Cambridge University (also father-in-law of the premier jockey, Frankie Dettori), Dr Robert Moor FRS and I, wrote and published

149

a book on 'The History of the Cambridge Animal Research Station' where we once worked. The book apart from biographies of research staff, research students and visitors, recalls fundamental studies carried out at the Station on domestic animals which have led to advances in animal breeding and human fertility: these include freezing of sperm and embryos, oral contraception, in vitro fertilization (IVF), cloning and embryo transfer; 'Dolly' the sheep arose from this work after Ian Wilmut (now Sir) left the Station in the early 1970's following a PhD on the freezing of boar sperm. Unfortunately the Animal Research Station was closed down in 1986 after over 50 years of research of global significance, due to government cuts, and the staff including me were absorbed into the Babraham Institute situated a few miles south of Cambridge.

My experience in pig breeding and an interest in the domestic pig's ancestor, the wild boar, led me to found the British Wild Boar Association in 1989 together with another zoologist, from Cambridge, Stephen Hall, an authority on rare breeds of farm animals, particularly Chillingham cattle. The aim of the association was to promote the alternative agricultural enterprise of wild boar farming in Britain which already occurred in Europe to add to the supply of the much sought after wild boar meat obtained from hunting the animal in the wild. Members of the British Wild Boar Association ranged from young existing farmers or those looking for a novel enterprise after having made money in another occupation, to aristocratic landowners and academics. However, the devastating gales of October 1987 resulted in trees being blown down across security fencing on wild boar farms and several animals escaped to the wild, particularly on the Kent and East Sussex border. It is a coincidence that probably the largest population of escaped wild boar in the UK are living in woods on the eastern edge of the Wealden hills in the area around Peasmarsh and Beckley – back to the haunts of 'Boy of the Wealden Shore'. There is also a significant population of escaped wild boar in the

Forest of Dean, a feature of several television documentaries.

The wild boar farmers were soon blamed for the escape of wild boar back to the wild in over 400 years when it was still then part of our natural fauna before being hunted to extinction. The concern was that the free living beast destroyed crops, is a carrier of pig diseases and a potential danger to the public, although the latter is an exaggerated concern, because the animal like deer tries to avoid people. These concerns have discouraged further increase in wild boar farming and I have retired from any involvement. The interest now is finding ways to control the feral population of wild boar and a research worker Martin Goulding has made a particular study of wild boar in the woods and countryside around Peasmarsh and Beckley. It will be interesting to see whether wild boar will become established in the wild again as a large game animal in Britain.

Another aspect of wild boar, is the beast in our heritage and its appearance in heraldry. A few years ago, a stained glass worker Alan Wright who by coincidence had a work shop in Elphinstone Road, Hastings, and unknown to me (although Alan's and my parents knew each other through attendance at St. Helen's Church), contacted me to show him some wild boar on a farm. The purpose of this was so that he could get the appearance correct for a stained glass window he had been contracted to make for the south aisle of York Minster. The window was a request from the Richard III Society and this king, previously a Duke of Gloucester, had been a keen hunter of wild boar and whose coat of arms included white wild boar. With my consultation, the window was duly completed and unveiled at a ceremony involving the present Duke of Gloucester.

More recently, I have had the opportunity to recapture my latent interest in local history and archaeology. I remember a school visit when I was at the Hastings Secondary Modern School for

Boys supervised by 'Puffer' Griffiths, a chain pipe smoker with lips bent to the side to hold the pipe, medium build with 'hedgehog' cut, grey hair, a blue corduroy jacket – more of a 'don' than a history teacher and my last form master at the school (knowing I was going to the Grammar School 'Puffer' lent me an introductory book to Latin called 'Latin with Laughter'; the introductory chapter was 'Vespa cantat', the 'Wasp sings'). We went to a building site along the High Street in the Old Town which revealed burnt timbers and brick in the soil being dug out for the foundations. This was the result of burning by the French when they ransacked the town in medieval times and my imagination was also fired seeing these events triggered by a few ashes – red and black, layered between different layers of soil as a 'time fix', what archaeologists refer to as 'stratification'.

Another antiquarian experience back in my childhood days in Hastings was when my friend Barry and I went for a cycle ride on our usual route for fishing to Snailham along the Rye Road, but on this Saturday afternoon we were just out for a ride in the country. Going up the hill out of Guestling in the direction of Rye, on our left up a track a couple of fields away, was a ruined cottage. Our curiosity got the better of us and we turned off the beaten track towards the cottage. When we got there, all that was left of the cottage were the crumbling walls, a few roof timbers and some timber joists for the first floor rooms. Barry and I gingerly climbed up on to the upper floor joists, then underneath a few remaining floor boards were scattered some necklace beads and a Victorian half penny in mint condition, dated 1853. My imagination was stirred to think that this half penny minted a 100 years earlier and the broken necklace may have laid under the floorboards since those days, lost by a child in their bedroom and being too frightened to tell the parents – a half penny was pocket money then and who knows how valuable the necklace was, materially or sentimentally?

Now, I have been involved as a volunteer with the Cambridgeshire professional archaeologists carrying out excavations and fieldwalks. This has led me into finding archaeological evidence for a Roman-British farmstead settlement, and further substantiating the supposed site of a 13th century manor house in fields close to our house in Milton. In parallel with this interest, I have been involved with the Cambridge Antiquarian Society (CAS), a 170 year old organization founded in the University of Cambridge to promote local history, archaeology and architectural history, but for the last 100 years it has embraced town's people as well, what we call in Cambridge a 'town and gown' organization. When I first became a member of CAS in 2000, monthly evening lectures were held in the Chemistry Laboratories where there was a large available lecture theatre; on entering the building we were confronted with photographs of past professors in the department. One of the most distinguished professors was ex-Hastings Grammar School boy H J Emeleus, professor of inorganic chemistry. H J together with his brother KG (who became a professor of physics at Queen's University, Belfast), came from an ex-Huguenot, Finnish family running a chemist's shop in Battle; these boys were two of the greatest scholars to be at the Grammar School in the early part of the 20th century. At the time of writing, another link between Cambridge and Hastings in the area of archaeology, is that Carenza Lewis currently President of CAS, was a 'Time Team' archaeologist working on the Roman bath and iron works site at Beauport Park just outside Hastings. This site had also been investigated by Gerald Brodribb who was born in St. Leonards-on-Sea, eventually went to Oxford University to read classics and English, played and wrote about cricket and became head master of Hydneye House School on The Ridge in Hastings; it was in retirement that he turned to archaeology.

In retirement, I have the opportunity as a husband, father of two daughters and grandfather to two grandsons to recapture some of the experiences of childhood from the other end of life's spectrum

153

within a family context. I grow vegetables for our two families on a village allotment, enjoy writing the occasional poem, painting, music and still occasionally go fishing; fortunately my legs can still take me on a walk or cycle ride. Like my childhood days in Hastings, all these interests evolve around living in a suburban community where I can still go 'Down the Town' for urban benefits, sometimes cycling the 3 miles from Milton to Cambridge along the tow path of the River Cam (unlike Hastings – no hills!), or to the woods and valleys to walk, cycle and fish and be with that everlasting aura of life – the natural world.

A final comment on bridging my childhood days spent in Hastings with the main part of my life spent in Cambridge. In 1865, a Finback whale was washed up on the beach at Pevensey and was displayed at the Central Cricket Ground in Hastings before the large skeleton was placed outside the zoology department in Cambridge University as seen today. Furthermore, Tom and Catherine Cookson travelled from Hastings to spend holidays on a boat in the Cambridgeshire fens; they cruised along the River Cam from Cambridge city to within half a mile of my house in Milton, but it was only after they died in 1998 that I became aware of this through reading their biographies. Catherine Cookson had travelled an even further journey from her earliest days of writing in Hastings (when she spoke about being a writer at my mother's young wives fellowship meeting at St. Helen's Church), to being rewarded with a global sale of her books, some dramatized in films, and she becoming a Dame of the British Empire. Bob Finch my botanist friend from Hastings Grammar School, also came to work and live in Cambridge, as mentioned earlier. Nowadays, I frequently see that other Old Hastonian friend, Brian Newbery ex-school teacher and watercolour artist who lives with his wife Maureen not far away in Letchworth. It is indeed a small world, circles within circles and there are many boys and girls who have gone out into the world, they also being 'Boys and Girls of the Wealden Shore', never to forget 1066 and all that!

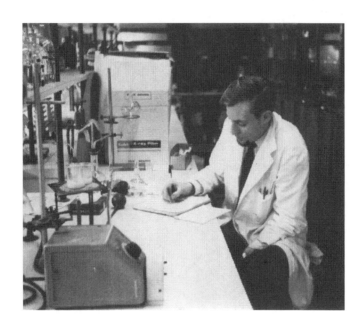

The author at University College Hospital Medical School,

London, Obstetric Research Unit (Endocrine Laboratories)

– planning the next experiment (1964)

The Animal Research Station, Cambridge.

The author's laboratory was behind the second windows from the right.

The Soay sheep were in addition to the more usual sheep, cattle, pigs

and horses held at the Station (1985)

"What do you think of my 'Andros' after shave dear?"

156

The Booth Family

Silver Wedding Anniversary

(1988)

Standing: Derek (the author)

Seated: L to R Judith, Catherine, Rebecca.

A small family herd of wild boar being farmed in a disused orchard.

Note the adult male (centre), sow behind and striped boarlets.

Roman pottery sherds from a field with a Romano-British

farmstead settlement near the author's house.

Top left: coarse grey ware; Top right: fine Nene ware;

Bottom left: fine Samian (red) ware; Bottom right: mortaria (a vessel for grinding herbs)

Concluding Thoughts

Anyone who has reached the eighth decade of life and was born at the beginning of the Second World War, has experienced a life of considerable social change in part due to the rapid acceleration in technical advances made in the last decades of the 20th century. I am one of these people, born in England whose humble ancestry can be traced back to East London, villages of Kent and East Sussex and subsequently Hastings in East Sussex where I spent my childhood. Apparently by coincidence, I have lived throughout my life in water ports either on the coast or inland, and in our heritage they have been important for communication, trade and progress.

My reflections on aspects of my childhood spent in Hastings, that seaside resort on the Wealden shore of the Sussex coast, are primarily confined to those which either influenced or impressed me most, including everyday experiences and those associated with my particular interests. Furthermore, how these interacted with the advancement of my education and my relationship with the family, friends and the wider public; this is the essence of 'Boy of the Wealden Shore'. There will be those who do not readily identify with my childhood experiences, either because they are more urban than me, or the opposite, have had a more rural childhood growing up on a farm, in a village or a child of fishermen at sea. Few can experience all these different backgrounds, but being a 'Boy of the Wealden Shore' living in suburbia, yet exposed to aspects of both rural and urban life, provided me along with others, a value added life.

Although my recall is undeniably autobiographical, the message I particularly wish to impart, is the social context of my childhood years which went beyond my own small world. In those years by comparison with today, life was simple, and in many ways easier to define. For example, the family both immediate and extended seemed to have a strong bonding, this bonding extended to local communities through schools, churches, trades, hobbies, sport and entertainment; fortunately today some of this social bonding still prevails in the smaller communities of villages and some urban areas. But, following the uncertain times of the Second World War, the recovery period afterwards in the late 1940's and 50's, was a period of great austerity, as it saw families re-united with their loved ones whether fathers returning from the battle front or evacuated children being returned to their parents; a continuing scene of a degree of self sufficiency prevailed.

One aspect of life over 50 years ago which was so different from today, was transport. Although the combustion engine had been invented at the end of the previous century, few people had private cars or motor cycles and therefore most people were restricted to public transport on buses or trains. The lack of private transport restricted many people to a limited environment for work and leisure, and in turn these activities were much less diverse than today. What I recall are activities which by comparison with today, particularly in the area of leisure, were relatively inexpensive. Childhood play for example, in woods and fields, or even specially landscaped recreation grounds, brought children together outside the classroom and in contact with nature. But today, although these facilities are still frequented by children, there has been a trend away from unorganized recreation in the outside world, to increased indoor leisure activities such as the use of computerized equipment associated with the television screen – some of these activities provide little mental or physical stimulation. In the 1940's and 50's older people's leisure was frequently spent outside, content to listen to a band in a park or on a seaside pier whether a local resident or a visitor. Then of course, whether young or old, with lack of mechanized transport, we were more dependent on our legs for walking or cycling, like me getting to school, doing a paper round or going on fishing trips into the countryside in all weathers – but it kept us fit.

One further comment on transport which made life over 50 years ago more sedentary and confined to our shores, was the lack of air transport. The expansion of air travel since those days is now so extensive that there a few people today who have not taken a holiday abroad by air; there are very few parts of the world that have not been 'invaded' by tourists whether the tops of high mountains, deserts, jungles or the Polar regions. In addition, people are routinely travelling by air on business, and food and other goods are being flown all round the globe.

Sources and nature of our food (contrary to that mentioned above) was also restricted during and after the War, but this resulted in people 'digging for victory'. More people grew their own vegetables and fruit in their back gardens, or rented allotments, and many also kept poultry and rabbits for eggs and meat; the rabbit skins were often treated for making children's gloves. However, today it is good to see an increasing interest again in growing your own fruit and vegetables, even keeping bees in both suburban and urban areas, despite the fact that with increasing affluence, eating out or retrieving food from 'take aways' has almost become 'the norm'. Eating out over 50 years ago was considered to be a really special occasion for most people apart from fish and chips, ice cream, cakes and sandwiches, or a 'fry up' in a snack bar – even this cheaper food was sometimes an associated treat with a holiday, and food in a public house was quite a rarity.

Another comparison between post War Britain and today is in the field of education. Leaving aside the topic of state versus private education, there has been a revolution in state secondary education in the last 50 years i.e. the creation of comprehensive schools. Before this was the universal 11 plus examination taken in the last

161

year of the primary school; this was to decide your fate as to whether you passed to follow a more academic path at a grammar school, or if you failed, to attend a secondary modern school of lesser academic standing with an emphasis on practical subjects. Being initially an 11 plus failure, then having the opportunity to have a 'second bite of the cherry' and to pass, I was one of the few who experienced both types of school, perhaps for a broader education, or just a waste of the first two years after primary school? On reflection, there were boys at the secondary modern school other than me who should not have failed their 11 plus, and vice versa, some boys at the grammar school were lucky to have passed this examination first time. The fact that I, and a few others had the opportunity to up-grade our education, was the seeding of the reform to introduce the comprehensive system. Furthermore, one's future based on one examination such as the 11 plus, has been generally replaced by continuous assessment schemes right through school to higher education, therefore providing a better assessment of an individuals ability; you only have to have an off day in well-being to lower your chances of passing an examination, and this could have a profound effect on the course of your life.

Before leaving the subject of education and comparing 50 years ago with today, if you obtained a batch of 'A' levels, 50 years ago to qualify you for university entrance, and you did not have private means to support the fees for a university education, you were provided with a local authority grant, or more rarely a grant from other sources. Today, with so many more students qualifying for university in keeping with the vast increase in the number of universities compared with half a century ago, there is now not enough money in the public purse to support all the students wishing to receive a university education. The consequence of this is that students have to seek loans of several thousands of pounds to enable them to attend university; this places a considerable burden on the students when they graduate, to pay back the loan over several years – to do this they must have a good job. But, the job must also supply income for general living and perhaps starting a family which needs to be housed in an adequate home with all the conveniences of the modern world. I am so grateful for the fact that I lived at a time when the government was still able to support students from ordinary homes, to go to university. Furthermore, we could make our grants go further because there were less material goods and entertainment to spend our money on.

My final thoughts are what does the future hold for Hastings? My reflections on the town in the 1940's and 50's reveal a different place to that seen today. Fifty years ago the town was still an important seaside resort, popular with visitors for its attractions as it had been since the coming of the railway in the first part of the 19th century. But with the advent of increased air travel since the 1960's, those who once spent their holiday at a British seaside resort, now go abroad to spend their time and money under the rays of more reliable sunshine. Sadly, my observations on the character of the town on the occasional visit in the last 40 years, seem to show more losses than gains. Where I lived in Hoad's Wood Road, has changed dramatically in the last 50 years. What was once a suburban hamlet surrounded by woods, ravines and farmland, is now joined to the town as the rural screen of Hoad's Wood and Scutes Farm have been replaced by housing and new roads; areas in the St. Helen's Wood area have likewise succumbed to houses and cul-de-sacs. However, new houses were needed and they had to be built somewhere. Furthermore, my second primary school, Mount Pleasant was demolished in the 1950's after I left, and replaced by housing; a new primary school Elphinstone School was opened in the Ore Valley which my brother and sister attended. Also my secondary modern school at Priory Road was closed following the adoption of the comprehensive system in Hastings, and the building converted into flats, following the same fate as my first primary school St. Andrews.

In the town, features such as the Albert Memorial situated at the hub of the main town have long since gone to be replaced by a plain junction of radial roads and pedestrian crossings. The salt water baths on the promenade, once of national fame and where I learned to swim while at school, have also gone – such a useful alternative when the weather was too bad to go on the beach; the same fate befell the open air Bathing Pool at St Leonards. The largest institution in land area was the Cricket Ground in the centre of the main town; this was a cricket pitch played on by Sussex and one of national repute; it is probably still a debatable issue as to whether this site should have succumbed to becoming a shopping centre? Another building, once seen from several views in the upper part of the town towards Alexandra Park was the old Grammar School which I attended. Soon after I left, the 1880's Grammar School building was demolished and replaced by a housing development; the only reminder of the School is the naming of the two closes, Saunders and Beckett after two of the school houses (I was in Saunders). Even if the school had to become a comprehensive school, the present William Parker School off St.Helen's Road, and expand its size, would not the old building have been useful as a sixth form college or other educational institution – perhaps a town library? Finally, at least one other dominant feature in the town has recently been thrown one step further towards extinction, that is the Victorian Pier, already disintegrating due to lack of responsible ownership – burnt down to its skeleton of iron supports in October 2010!

Social evolution must go on, perhaps I am being over pessimistic because there is still hope that some of the heritage of Hastings can be restored or enhanced. Western-super-Mare pier has recently been wonderfully restored after being burnt down a few years ago, let's hope Hastings Pier can have the same resurrection with the return of a large pavilion for musical and other entertainment events requiring a covered area with refreshment facilities (jazz festivals are a great pull to St Ives in Cornwall);

indoor sports facilities might also be considered. Perhaps a passenger boat can be reinstated (I remember a paddle steamer providing trips just after the War) at the end of the Pier for trips along the coast – splendid views west to the South Downs and the Wealden shore and cliffs before Rye Bay to the east. Other cultural attractions are actually underway with the prospect of an important modern art gallery being built on the Stade in the Old town as part of the 'Stade Project'. There is also the advent of The Hastings Seafood Festival which could be a prelude to establishing seafood restaurants – why should the French do this and not us? We both share the same water, the English Channel with its wealth of white fish and shell fish and we have a built in fishing industry already in place with a need to expand, do we not? But, I am optimistic that the town will move in a positive direction with new attractions that will replace some of its lost heritage and prospects for higher education with the opening of degree awarding colleges which are now underway.

Leaving aside regional and debatable cultural differences, there is one very positive asset Hastings and its environs has to offer, and that is its rich natural landscape formed from the Wealden hills as they fall away to the flat river valleys and pasture lands with Romney Marsh to the east and the Pevensey levels to the west, to the south is the Wealden shore. The Hastings Country Park, the preservation of St. Helen's Wood and Alexandra Park add to the wild life context while the numerous castles and old buildings and monuments in this part of Sussex provide an equally rich historic landscape. We live in an age when there is still too much ignorance of our wildlife. The newspaper, The Daily Telegraph recently reported the following in this regard: less than 25% of British people could identify a sycamore tree and over 60% could not recognize a peacock butterfly in a survey for the Natural History Museum. 60% of people could identify a toad, but 30% thought it was a frog, and only 20% recognized an ammonite, Britain's most common fossil; there were still 30% of people who did not recognize a woodlouse. Dr Johannes Vogel of the Museum said, "It's a real shame how little, people seem to understand the natural world". I fully support this comment and I know that the environs of Hastings are there to correct this deficit – it is free to all to see and hear. I benefited from this inspiring part of England as I have endeavoured to illustrate in 'Boy of the Wealden Shore', I hope others have had, or will have a similar rewarding experience.

Muriel Hilton has aptly captured in her poem, boyhood spent in Sussex, and thoughts that might pass through the minds of those boys who grow up and leave the rural county for other places.

"Sussex Scene"

These happy boys that wend their way
Through shining buttercups of gold,
Will they remember these fair fields,
These meadow lands when they are old?

If they remember, will it be
With vain regrets and bitter tears,
That they have gathered other gold,
But lost the rapture through the years?

© Muriel Hilton

'Out of Season'

Can the promenade continue to draw the crowds?

Note: centre, South African War Memorial; centre left,

entrance building to earlier swimming baths (May 2008)

Will the Pier be restored to its former glory after the fire

of October 2010?

© Brian Newbery

The 'Boy' (the author) returns to the Wealden Shore

at Fairlight in the Hastings Country Park, in 2009.

Further Reading

Anderton, Stephen: *Christopher Lloyd (His Life at Great Dixter)*. Chatto & Windus, London, (2010).

Booth, W.D.: *A Preliminary Account of the Littoral (intertidal) Fauna and Flora at Ecclesbourne, near Hastings.* The Hastings Naturalist Vol.X, No.3, edit. L.R. Conisbee, (1966). [with the assistance of R.A Finch – also includes the effect of the town's sewage into the sea on shore life].

Brodribb, Gerald: *Hastings and Men of Letters.* Old Hastings Preservation Society, (1971).
[includes Catherine Cookson and Warwick Deeping].

Brooks, Ken: *Geology and Fossils of the Hastings Area.* Published by Ken Brooks, (2001).
[notably the coast from Rock-a-Nore to Pett Level].

Bullock, F.W.B.: *Ruins of the Old Parish Church of St. Helen, Ore, Sussex.* (1949). [includes many old prints of the church in earlier landscapes, but out of print].

Cardwell, Tony: *Limen. A biography of the East Sussex Rother.* The Wealden Advertiser Ltd., Cowden Lane, Horns Road, Hawkhurst, Kent TN18 4QT.

Coates, Geoff: *Memories of Early Hastings Jazz " We heard ya talkin".* Calle Cordoba 6, Torrox, Malaga, 29770, Spain, (2002). [Geoff Coates was the banjo and guitar player with the Dolphin Jazz Band].

Dudgeon, Piers: *Kate's Daughter (the real Catherine Cookson).* Bantam Press, Transworld Publishers, 61-68 Uxbridge Road, London W5 5SA, (2003). [includes reference to Tom Cookson and the Hastings Grammar School in more detail than other biographies].

Dudgeon, Piers: *The Life and Writing of Catherine Cookson (The Girl from Leam Lane).* Headline Publishing Group, 338 Euston Road, London NW1 3BH, (2007). [revised and expanded centenary edition].

Gallois,R.W. & Edmunds, F.H.: *The Wealden District* (4th edition). Her Majesty's Stationary Office, (1965). [a geological review including the Wealden shore from Hastings to Pett Level].

Goodwin, Nathan Dylan: H*astings at War 1939-1945.* Philliman & Co. Ltd., Shopwyke Manor Barn, Chichester, West Sussex, England, (2005). [a good overview with reference to the evacuation of the Hastings Grammar School to St. Albans].

Goulding, Martin: *Wild Boar in Britain.* Whittet Books Ltd, Hill Farm, Stonham Road, Cotton, Stowmarket, Suffolk IP14 4RQ, (2003). [history, biology and natural history, future status].

Green, John: *From a Country Rectory Window.* The Rectory, Sandhurst, Kent, (1990). ['Jottings of a Wealden Parson' – Rev. John Green past rector of St. Nicholas Church, Sandhurst].

Hilton, Muriel: *Sussex Days.* Published by the Rev. Denbigh Hilton, 45 Hoad's Wood Road, Hastings, (circa 1945). [Muriel and Denbigh deceased, no further association with above address].

Hilton, Muriel: *The Magic of Common Things.* Wayside Special Books – No.6. The Epworth Press, 25-35 City Road, London EC1, (1949).

Hilton, Muriel: *The Charm of the Common Place.* Wayside Special Books – No.11. The Epworth Press, 25-35 City Road, London EC1 (1951).

Hodges, John: *Hastings a Bibliography.* The Old Hastings Preservation Society, (2008).

Hutchison, Geoff: *Grey Owl (The Hastings Indian).* Published by Geoff Hutchison, (2005).

Kynaston, David: *Austerity Britain 1945-51.* Bloomsbury Publishing Plc. 36 Soho Square, London W1D 3QY, (2007).

Lawes, Brian: *Twittens, Passages and Steps.* Published by Hastings History House, 21 Courthouse Street, Hastings, (2010).

Manwaring Baines, J. and Conisbee, L.R.: *The History of the Hastings Grammar School, 1619-1956.* The Governors of the Hastings Grammar School Foundation, (1956). [revised edition including author (ex-master) N.Bygate, 1967]

Manwaring Baines, J.: *Historic Hastings.* F.J.Parsons Ltd.,

Observer Buildings, Cambridge Road, Hastings, (1969).

Marchant, Rex: *Hastings Past.* Phillimore & Co. Ltd, (1997).
[includes an excellent photograph of 'Boag'].

Padgham, David: *The Archaeology & History of Hastings Country Park.* Hastings Area Archaeological Research Group, (2006).

Peak, Steve: *Fishermen of Hastings (200 years of the Hastings Fishing Industry).* Published by Steve Peak, 36 Collier Road, Hastings, East Sussex TN34 3JR, (2005).

Peak, Steve: *Mugsborough Revisited (author Robert Tressell and the setting of his famous book, 'The Ragged Trousered Philanthropists').* Published by Steve Peak, 36 Collier Road, Hastings, East Sussex TN34 3JR, (2011).

Preston, Edward: *St. Helen's Park 50 Years On.* Literatours, 63 Bohemia Road, St. Leonards-on-
Sea, East Sussex TN37 6RG, (2010). [references to founders of the St. Helen's Park Preservation Society Ltd., including Tom and Catherine Cookson – several good site photographs].

Ridd, Jenny: *A Destiny Defined (Dante Gabriel Rossetti and Elizabeth Siddal in Hastings).* Edgerton Publishing Services, Pett, East Sussex TN35 4JD, (2008). [these Pre-Raphaelite artists married at St. Clements Church, Hastings. William Holman Hunt was another of these artists with Hastings connections].

Salzman, L.F.: *The Victoria History of the County of Sussex. Vol.9, The Rape of Hastings.* The University of London, Institute of Historical Research, (1973). [details of historic buildings – churches, castles, estates in the Hastings area].

Seymour, Victoria: *The Long Road To Lavender Cottage.* Published by Victoria Seymour, 33 Greville Road, Hastings, East Sussex TN35 5AL, (2006). [social history of people and places particularly in The Ridge area from Baldslow to Ore – many of these known to the 'Boy of the Wealden Shore'].

Seymour, Victoria: *The Slow Turning Tide (Hastings in Austerity 1946-1954).* Published by Victoria Seymour, 33 Greville Road, Hastings, East Sussex TN35 5AL, (2008). [biographies in the social historical context of Hastings].

Seymour, Victoria: *Victory's Children (Hastings 1945-2010)*. Published by Victoria Seymour, 33 Greville Road, Hastings, East Sussex TN35 5AL, (2010). [biographies in the social historical context of Hastings].

Note: The following books by Victoria Seymour are also relevant to the period of World War II to the present day. *Letters to Hannah; Court in the Act; Letters to Lavender Cottage; Austerity Diary from Lavender Cottage, Hastings, 1947*.

Strong, Patience: *Life is for Living*. Frederick Muller Ltd., (1975). [this author is buried in the churchyard of St. Nicholas, Sandhurst, Kent, near the grave of the 'Boy of the Wealden Shore's' eldest daughter Amanda].